Take This Cup

Take This Cup

How God Transforms Suffering into Glory and Joy

CHARLES ERLANDSON

WIPF & STOCK · Eugene, Oregon

TAKE THIS CUP
How God Transforms Suffering into Glory and Joy

Copyright © 2020 Charles Erlandson. All rights reserved. Except for brief quotations in critical publications or reviews, no part of this book may be reproduced in any manner without prior written permission from the publisher. Write: Permissions, Wipf and Stock Publishers, 199 W. 8th Ave., Suite 3, Eugene, OR 97401.

Scripture taken from the New King James Version. Copyright © 1982 by Thomas Nelson, Inc. Used by permission. All rights reserved.

Wipf & Stock
An Imprint of Wipf and Stock Publishers
199 W. 8th Ave., Suite 3
Eugene, OR 97401

www.wipfandstock.com

PAPERBACK ISBN: 978-1-7252-6203-4
HARDCOVER ISBN: 978-1-7252-6201-0
EBOOK ISBN: 978-1-7252-6204-1

Manufactured in the U.S.A.   04/27/20

To my wife, Jackie,
who is my own personal Simon of Cyrene.

"So Jesus said to them, You will indeed drink the cup that I drink..."
(MARK 10:39)

CONTENTS

Preface	ix
THE FIRST CUP: WE REJECT THE CUP WHICH GOD OFFERS	1
THE SECOND CUP: CHRIST TAKES THE CUP FOR US	7
THE SECOND CUP, PART I: CHRIST TOOK THE CUP	9
Chapter 1: God's Goodness and the Existence of Evil	11
Chapter 2: God Showed His Love by Taking on Human Nature	15
Chapter 3: Jesus Took on Human Suffering	18
Chapter 4: Jesus Has Transformed the Meaning of Suffering	29
Chapter 5: Suffering Is How We See God	37
THE SECOND CUP, PART II: UNION WITH CHRIST BY SUFFERING	43
Chapter 1: Christ Shares His Human Nature with the Church	45
Chapter 2: We Are United to Christ Through Baptism	53
Chapter 3: Baptized Christians are United to All of Christ	58
Chapter 4: The Eucharistic Body, Holy Communion, and Suffering: What God has Joined Together, Let Not Man Separate	63
Chapter 5: Suffering Is a Sacrament of Christ's Presence	74
Chapter 6: Jesus Took on All Human Suffering which He Distributes Throughout His Body	76
THE SECOND CUP, PART III: CHRISTIAN SUFFERING UNITES US TO JESUS CHRIST AND, THEREFORE, BRINGS US GLORY AND JOY	85
Chapter 1: God Commands and Promises Glory and Joy through Suffering	87
Chapter 2: Suffering Unites Us to the Source of All Joy	96

Chapter 3: We Partake of Christ's Victory Over His Enemies   99
Chapter 4: We have been Counted Worthy to Partake of
God's Redemption   104
Chapter 5: God is Treating Us as His Children   109
Chapter 6: Suffering Transforms Us into the Image of Christ   113
Chapter 7: Suffering Unites Us to One Another   119
Chapter 8: We Suffer for the Good of Others   125
Chapter 9: Suffering Is an Angel and the World's Greatest
Mnemonic Device   139
Chapter 10: You Can't Have a Resurrection without a Crucifixion   144
Chapter 11: Suffering is a Measure of God and Man   149
Chapter 12: Our Suffering Brings God Glory   153

THE THIRD CUP: OUR OFFERING OF OURSELVES TO GOD   159
Chapter 1: Introduction   161
Chapter 2: We Take This Cup, in the Garden, Praying the Lord's Prayer   163
Chapter 3: God Is Redeeming Man by Man   169
Chapter 4: We Offer Our Cup of Suffering to the Father   172
Chapter 5: We Take the Cup and Find Christ in It   179

Appendix: Joy and Glory in Other Passages   183
Bibliography   193
Subject Index   195
Scripture Index   201

PREFACE

There seemed to be no use in waiting by the little door, so she went back to the table, half hoping she might find another key on it, or at any rate a book of rules for shutting people up like telescopes: this time she found a little bottle on it ("which certainly was not here before," said Alice), and round the neck of the bottle was a paper label, with the words "DRINK ME" beautifully printed on it in large letters.

It was all very well to say "Drink me," but the wise little Alice was not going to do that in a hurry. "No, I'll look first," she said, "and see whether it's marked 'poison' or not"; for she had read several nice little histories about children who had got burnt, and eaten up by wild beasts and other unpleasant things, all because they would not remember the simple rules their friends had taught them: such as, that a red-hot poker will burn you if you hold it too long; and that if you cut your finger very deeply with a knife, it usually bleeds; and she had never forgotten that, if you drink much from a bottle marked "poison," it is almost certain to disagree with you, sooner or later.

However, this bottle was NOT marked "poison," so Alice ventured to taste it, and finding it very nice (it had, in fact, a sort of mixed flavour of cherry-tart, custard, pine-apple, roast turkey, toffee, and hot buttered toast), she very soon finished it off.

"What a curious feeling!" said Alice; "I must be shutting up like a telescope."

And so it was indeed: she was now only ten inches high, and her face brightened up at the thought that she was now the right size for going though the little door into that lovely garden.

In this book, I am asking you to join me on an adventure very much like Alice's adventure in Wonderland and very much not like Alice's adventure in Wonderland.

Preface

I'm asking you to raise a very special glass with me, offered not by me but by Another. Like Alice, a vessel is offered to us, saying in effect, "Drink Me."

This cup was indeed once a cup of deadly poison, as Alice suspected it might be, but we are the ones who have deposited the poison in the potion. When we drink it, as we must, we should all die, and not merely shrink. But the cup and its contents have been transformed, and that which once brought death now offers life, and life abundantly beyond all imagining.

The cup, or, more properly, the contents of the cup, are whispering, speaking, and shouting at us. For the One saying "Drink Me" is Jesus Christ, and the cup he is offering us is his very own cup, the cup of suffering.

This Holy Grail was never really lost, just overlooked, for like Poe's purloined letter, we have been looking for it in all the wrong places.

This cup is a mysterious cup. It is the strangest, sourest, sweetest, most transmutational, most potent cup on earth. It is the cup of suffering. And if we drink it with Christ, like Alice, we will never be the same, for the cup will change us.

But it will only transmute us into who we are meant to be if we take it from and with Jesus Christ. For to take the cup of suffering with Jesus is to become one with Jesus in his death and resurrection.

WHY ME?

Everyone who has ever suffered (which is everyone) has asked this question. God must want us to ask this question, because in seeking to comprehend suffering we are seeking God, often without knowing it.

Why am I afflicted with this terrible weakness? Why can't I have energy like everyone else and like I used to have?

Why me?

To ask "Why Me?" is to ask, "What is the meaning of human suffering?"

This book is my answer, and, I believe and hope, the biblical answer to this question.

In a way, I'm offering a Christian theodicy—a vindication of God's goodness in light of the existence of evil and suffering. But my theodicy, my meditation on how God brings the good of glory and joy out of the evil of suffering, will only make sense, I'm afraid, to Christians.

For the answer to theodicy is partaking of Christ—apart from this, all merely logical answers will be unsatisfactory.

God Himself does not directly answer our human questions about theodicy and suffering. What he does instead is far better: he offers up his Son for and to us, to take our suffering into himself and transform it into glory and joy.

I have written this book that you might believe that your suffering has a meaning and that this meaning is a good one.

I have written this book that you might know that God is good.

I have written this book that you might rejoice in your suffering because all Christian suffering unites us to Jesus Christ and, therefore, leads to glory and joy.

I make this audacious, and even offensive, claim because it is the Good News of Jesus Christ proclaimed in a different way. It is the Good News that God is good and is taking care of human suffering by taking it on himself and sharing himself with us. It is what I will be calling "The Gospel of Suffering."

It is the Good News that God takes what men and devils mean for evil and transforms it into our glory and joy, through his Son.

So, take this cup and drink it with Christ and me, for drinking with someone is almost always a kind of celebration or feast, a time for joy and good feeling. Drinking together rejoices the heart and creates a bond of deepest fellowship.

In no way do I want to minimize the pain and suffering you, or those you love, are experiencing. But only if we first acknowledge the awful evil of suffering will we be in a position to experience glory and joy as we see God in our suffering as he transforms it.

THE FIRST CUP

We Reject the Cup Which God Offers

This book is a tale of three cups.

1. The first part is about how God offers us the cup of suffering, and we reject it.
2. The second part is about how God offers the cup of suffering to his Son, who takes it for us.
3. The third and final part is about how, with Christ, we now take the cup and receive in it both him and his blessings of glory and joy.

TAKE THIS CUP: THE REJECTION OF SUFFERING

They say that nothing is certain except death and taxes. We might add, "Nothing is universal except human suffering." The Buddha began with this one great insight: all life is suffering. His draconian remedy was to extinguish desire, which was, in his mind, the cause of suffering.

So heavy, so painful, so destructive is human suffering that man has devised many pain-management techniques and strategies over the centuries. Some turn to religion, such as Buddhism. Some turn to the bottle or needle or bong. Some become stoics or rageaholics or crusaders. And some shrivel up and slowly die.

Few have ever thought of truly embracing their suffering because we know that suffering is evil and naturally want to avoid it. Some have come to the "Aha!" moment of seeing a limited use for suffering in making us tougher, more resilient people, and yet we know this is not enough.

What a glorious shock to discover a God who becomes man precisely to suffer! How joyful to discover a God who continues to delight in hiding himself in suffering as he conquers it from within!

For reasons related to our own sin and God's desire to redeem us from our sin and its consequences, God offers us the cup of suffering. Unseen as God himself is the fact that this cup (because it is attached to his beloved Son) is also the cup of salvation. But many, even Christians, will refuse the suffering God providentially allows us.

For suffering is a sign of sin and the death that is, for man, the wages of his sin. So offensive is suffering, so terrible and mighty, that even Christians who have received God's promises about how he will use suffering for good experience great difficulty in comprehending or accepting suffering.

When God says to us, "Take this cup of suffering," most of us will push the cup away.

THE REJECTION OF THE CUP BY JESUS'S DISCIPLES

Like us, Jesus's disciples rejected the cup, pushed it away, and were unable to take it, until the Day of Pentecost. Mark 8–10 reveals how difficult it was even for Jesus's disciples to comprehend and accept the cross.

In Mark 8, Peter confessed Jesus as the Christ. Immediately, after Peter's confession, Jesus

> began to teach them that the Son of Man must suffer many things, and be rejected by the elders and chief priests and scribes, and be killed, and after three days rise again. He spoke this word openly. Then Peter took Him aside and began to rebuke Him. But when He had turned around and looked at His disciples, He rebuked Peter, saying, "Get behind Me, Satan! For you are not mindful of the things of God, but the things of men" (Mark 8:31–33).

At the very moment of Peter's great confession of Christ (which most of us remember), Satan is lurking at his door with temptation (which many of us forget). Jesus's self-revelation of himself as Messiah was synonymous with his self-revelation of himself as the Suffering Servant who must go to Jerusalem to die and be raised from the dead. The gospel of Jesus Christ is the Gospel of Suffering. And Peter rejected it.

Jesus's very next teaching was this: "Whoever desires to come after Me, let him deny himself, and take up his cross, and follow Me. For whoever desires to save his life will lose it, but whoever loses his life for My sake and the gospel's will save it" (Mark 8:34–35). Already, Jesus has connected his own suffering and death with the suffering and death of his disciples. Jesus's cross will become the crosses of his disciples.

WAYS WE REJECT THE CUP

Jesus's disciples today still push away the cup of suffering, which Christ himself offers us.

How do we do this?

Martin Luther spoke of a theology of glory, an attempt to partake of the blessings of God apart from suffering. Luther contrasted this to the theology of the cross, which is God-centered and clings to the necessity of the cross for Christians.

Contemporary Christian theologies which attempt to minimize the necessity of the cross—not just for Christ but also for Christians—may be termed theologies of glory. Those who preach the prosperity gospel, the health and wealth gospel, the name it and claim it gospel, and the self-help gospel are all preaching theologies of glory. These are all attempts to attract the blessing of God without the suffering and sacrifice of giving oneself entirely to God. Theologies that see the primary good of suffering in its ability to make us stronger and more resilient people are also theologies of glory.

The theology of glory is also present whenever Christians turn primarily to politics and political parties to be their saviors. The urge to seek and attribute to the state the blessings of God, such as health, wealth, and liberty, is a theology of glory. Likewise, the urge to focus on the good and achievements of individuals instead of communities may also become a theology of glory.

Christians may follow the culture in medicating or intoxicating away the problem of suffering. This "lipstick on a pig" approach to suffering includes the numbing or distracting from suffering through virtual life in social media, eating or amusing ourselves to death, or other essentially hedonistic prescriptions. Workaholism, ultimately, has the same goal and effect.

Even our worship can become a rejection of the cup, leaving no place for a painful confession of sins but instead measuring the value of a worship experience by how we feel after going to it. Too often, we want the feast without the fast; Easter without Good Friday; and life in Christ without dying to self.

In all these ways and more, Christians reject the cup of suffering which Jesus offers them.

We say, "take this cup away," along with Jesus's first-century disciples, not realizing that to reject the cup is to reject the Christ who offers it and whose blood is in it.

CHRIST'S TEMPTATION TO REFUSE THE CUP

Jesus, being fully human, was also tempted, as all men are, to reject the cup the Father offered. He did not escape either suffering or the temptation to flee from the suffering God had assigned him.

Jesus's own temptation to reject the cup of suffering began not in the garden but in the wilderness. Each of Satan's temptations in the wilderness was an offering of a Christ without a cross.

"Why are you fasting, Jesus?" Satan insinuated. "Why are you depriving yourself of things to which you have a right? Haven't you hungered enough for man? Take the stones which you created, and make them bread. This will be good practice for when you want to persuade the crowds of who you are: surely, they'll be impressed when you multiply bread, and, surely, they'll listen when you fill their bellies. You know that you can save man without suffering fully as a man, don't you?"

"Throw yourself down from the pinnacle of the temple. You'll get credit for being brave and courageous, and yet you'll know that there's no real threat to you. You know, even if these humans don't, that your angels will never let you die and will come and rescue you before you hit the earth. And what a spectacle for all who may be watching! What confirmation they'll have of your superhuman courage and the power of God. This is just the kind of sacrifice that's needed: dramatic, heroic, and yet utterly safe in the end."

"Here are all of the kingdoms of the world that the Father has promised you. You can have them now, and for only a nominal price. You can rule them all, no strings attached, if only you'll fall down and worship me.

We Reject the Cup Which God Offers

You don't even have to really mean it: you just have to do it. No one will be the wiser. You'll get to rule, you'll have your promised glory, but it will be so much easier for everyone this way. Who knows, but that this is God's appointed way?"

Jesus, in his humanity, naturally recoiled from the immeasurable suffering set before him, and he was tempted to reject it. This is especially evident in the temptation in the Garden of Gethsemane. "Father, if it is Your will, take this cup away from Me" (Luke 22:42) was Jesus's threefold prayer. "And being in agony, He prayed more earnestly. Then His sweat became like great drops of blood falling down to the ground" (Luke 22:44).

The Son prayed, "Father, if it is Your will, take this cup away from Me," but he also prayed, "nevertheless not My will, but Yours, be done" (Luke 22:42).

And so on the cross, Jesus took the cup of all human suffering, the cup of sin and death.

But Satan was not done yet with his temptations. Even on the cross, Jesus was tempted to wish the cup away. "And those who passed by blasphemed Him, wagging their heads and saying, 'You who destroy the temple and build *it* in three days, save Yourself! If You are the Son of God, come down from the cross'" (Matt 27:39–40).

Several temptations are mixed in this potion of seduction. Take the easy way out: if you save yourself, people will believe even more than if you die. Isn't the whole point to demonstrate the power of life over death and that you are the high and mighty ruler who can do whatever he wants and is stronger than even the Romans?

There is the temptation of taunting. Who among us hasn't bristled at an insult, become enraged, and wanted to take immediate and violent action?

There's the doubt that would undoubtedly be planted in the minds of many if Jesus permitted himself to die: what a display of weakness for the Son of God this would be. "He saved others; Himself He cannot save. If He is the King of Israel, let Him now come down from the cross, and we will believe Him" (Matt 27:42). There you have it: if you come down from the cross right now, men will believe, but if you allow yourself to be put to death, no one will believe.

But Jesus resolved to take the cup for us.

Having taken the cup for us, Jesus offers it to us, but only because he is attached to it, in his kingdom, his power, and his glory.

The First Cup

O sacred head, sore wounded,
Defiled and put to scorn:
O kingly head, surrounded
With mocking crown of thorn;
What sorrow mars thy grandeur?
Can death thy bloom deflow'r?
O countenance whose splendor
The hosts of heav'n adore!

Thy beauty, long desired,
Hath vanished from our sight:
Thy pow'r is all expired,
And quenched the light of light.
Ah me! for whom thou diest,
Hide not so far thy grace:
Show me, O Love most highest,
The brightness of thy face.

In thy most bitter passion
My heart to share doth cry.
With thee for my salvation
Upon the cross to die.
Ah, keep my heart thus moved
To stand thy cross beneath,
To mourn thee, well-beloved,
Yet thank thee for thy death.

What language shall I borrow
To thank thee, dearest friend,
For this thy dying sorrow,
Thy pity without end?
Oh, make me thine forever!
And should I fainting be,
Lord, let me never, never
Outlive my love for thee.

My days are few, O fail not,
With thine immortal pow'r,
To hold me that I quail not
In death's most fearful hour:
That I may fight befriended,
And see in my last strife
To me thine arms extended
Upon the cross of life. (Paul Gerhardt, translated by Robert Bridges)

THE SECOND CUP

Christ Takes the Cup for Us

INTRODUCTION TO THE SECOND CUP

God offered us himself in the garden of Eden, and we refused him, leading to our expulsion from the paradise of God.

But God so loved the world that he sent his only begotten Son. Jesus Christ, the Son of God, takes the cup on our behalf so that with, in, by, through, and for him, we can now also take the cup. The way back to paradise is purchased at the terrible price of the life of the Son of God, who took the cup for us.

The Father says to his beloved Son: "Take this cup of human suffering, sin, and death, which every man, and especially all men together, deserve. Take this cup, even though they are the ones who deserve it, and transform their evil into good. Take this cup that they might live."

Knowing precisely the lethal price it will cost him, the Son says, "I will. I will take this cup."

Jesus took the cup that we might, with him, take the cup. He has not asked us to do something He has not first done for us. When we say "I will" with the Son, something miraculous happens! We discover the thesis of this book, which is only the teaching of the Scriptures: what I will be calling the gospel of suffering.

In its simplest form, the gospel of suffering proclaims this: that suffering is God's means by which, united to Jesus, we experience joy and glory in the presence of God.

More formally, we may express the gospel of suffering in these three interrelated truths, which will be presented in the three major sections of the second cup:

1. Far from being a sign of God's nonexistence, apathy, or impotence, human suffering is transformed by Christ into a sign of God's presence, love, and power.

2. Because Christ has become man and suffered to redeem man, suffering is a primary means of participating in God's nature and being united to him.

3. As Christians partake of Christ and his suffering, their own suffering is transformed by God into glory and joy.

THE SECOND CUP, PART I

Christ Took the Cup

FAR FROM BEING A sign of God's nonexistence, apathy, or impotence, human suffering is transformed by Christ into a sign of God's presence, love, and power.

CHAPTER 1

God's Goodness and the Existence of Evil

Let us begin, as always, with God. I will begin with the simplest and boldest of assertions, one that was frequently taken for granted in the past but is frequently assumed to be false today: God is good (Matt 19:17).

This is not just to say that God is generically good or that whatever he decrees is good, regardless of what he does. God is inherently good, and since God's existence and essence are one (who he is, is what he does), God always *does* good things. God is *simple* in this way. Because God is good, he created the world good, proclaiming after each day of the creation that what he had created was good.

What do we mean by "good"? I will assume that something is good if it brings glory to God and blesses (or "does good to") man and creation.

God is good, and he loves the world. The Holy Trinity is an eternal fellowship of divine love between the Father, the Son, and the Holy Spirit. Just as God *is* good, God *is* love and, therefore, always does loving things. In fact, a good definition of love is to seek the good and blessing of another—the very thing that God always does.

The act of creation, then, is an act of love because to call good things into existence is to do them good and bless them. In this way, the creation reveals the glory of God by his love.

It is more difficult to define evil and suffering. But we must define them before we can fully comprehend and accept the truth that God has sent his Son to triumph over evil and suffering and transform them into blessing and joy. Our implicit understanding of evil and suffering may sometimes limit our ability to comprehend suffering.

One of Saint Augustine's many brilliant insights was to understand that evil is not a thing in and of itself but is a perversion or deprivation of some good.[1] It is a parasite on good and does not exist by itself. Man suffers when he experiences any evil: in fact, suffering and evil are closely related throughout the Old Testament. More particularly, we can say that suffering is the lack of some good thing of which someone has been deprived.

Suffering, therefore, is universally present in men, and this suffering takes many forms. It's not limited to the physical and emotional suffering we most commonly think of: we suffer any time we are deprived of the good for which God has created us.

This is the definition of evil and suffering I'll be assuming throughout *Take This Cup*: "We suffer any time we experience evil, which is the deprivation of the good for which God created us."

These evil causes of suffering may be either moral evil or natural evil.

Moral evil is suffering caused by men acting in morally wrong ways

Natural evil is suffering caused by events not caused by man, such as earthquakes, tornadoes, etc.

The truth is that moral evil is not only more prevalent than men will admit but also infects much more of the world than men discern. How often have we failed to recognize our part in someone else's suffering or failed to take responsibility for our participation in moral evil?!

Many people have honest questions about human suffering. Many also assume that suffering is a proof that God doesn't exist or is not good or powerful enough to do something about human suffering. But God does exist, he is loving and good, and he has powerfully done something about human suffering.

And what he has done is to send his Son into the world to take on human nature, suffer for us, and redeem this suffering. "*For God so loved the world that He gave His only begotten Son, that whoever believes in Him should not perish but have everlasting life*" (John 3:16).

When sin, evil, and suffering entered into the world, God did not sit idly by and watch his children suffer. In the fullness of time, God the Father decisively entered into human suffering and showed his Fatherly love by

---

1. I'm aware both of other understandings of the nature of evil and also of objections to Augustine's theory. However, it seems to be the most useful way of seeing evil as we attempt to understand suffering.

sending his Son to take on human nature *and its suffering*, redeem human nature, and restore it to union with him.

In assuming human nature to redeem it, God revealed his essential goodness. God is, indeed, very good—so good that his nature is always to take evil and transform it into good. As Joseph told his brothers, whose evil had caused him so much suffering: "But as for you, you meant evil against me; *but* God meant it for good, to bring it about as *it is* this day, to save many people alive" (Gen 50:20).

This is the cornerstone of the thesis of this book: that God takes what men and devils mean for evil and turns it into good.

Let me emphasize that while God brings good out of evil and suffering, suffering itself is a form of evil. There is no doubt about it: suffering, in itself, is ugly, shameful, and painful. I should also stress that responding to suffering with faith and submission to God will not necessarily lessen the suffering, although its meaning will be radically transformed. Suffering will not automatically sanctify a person, including a Christian, if the suffering is not received with Christ in faith.

It is precisely because suffering is so terrible that God's transformation of it into our good is so miraculous and such a potent sign of God, his power, and his love. Love is doing good to others; therefore, love undoes the evil of sin and suffering. But this also means that love, in undoing suffering, partakes of suffering. For love means giving up one's own good for the good of another.

Let us look next at how Jesus has entered into human suffering and offers himself and his suffering on behalf of us.

> *Glory be to Jesus,*
> *who, in bitter pains,*
> *poured for me the life-blood*
> *from his sacred veins!*
>
> *Grace and life eternal*
> *in that blood I find;*
> *blest be his compassion*
> *infinitely kind!*
>
> *Blest thro' endless ages*
> *be the precious stream*
> *which from endless torments*
> *did the world redeem!*

The Second Cup, Part I

Abel's blood for vengeance
pleaded to the skies;
but the blood of Jesus
for our pardon cries.

Oft as earth exulting
wafts its praise on high,
angel hosts rejoicing
make their glad reply.

Lift we, then, our voices,
swell the mighty flood,
louder still and louder
praise the precious blood!
(eighteenth-century Italian, translated by Edward Caswall)

CHAPTER 2

God Showed His Love by Taking on Human Nature

God showed his Fatherly love by sending his Son to take on human nature and its suffering, that he might redeem it and restore it to union with him, a union which always leads to glory and joy.

When God chose to become man, he also chose to unite himself to all human suffering.

That is to say: Christ's incarnation is inseparable from his crucifixion (and also that both of these are inseparable from his resurrection, ascension, and gift of the Holy Spirit). Before we meditate more deeply on the manifold sufferings of Christ, let us first pause briefly to consider his incarnation.

At the incarnation, Jesus assumed a human nature so that in him, the divine and human natures are united. The two natures of Christ are, according to the Council of Chalcedon (451), *"without confusion, without change, without division, and without separation."* This is what is sometimes called the hypostatic union, or union of "natures." In the incarnation, the Son of God *assumed* human nature: He was *not changed into* it. As the early church father, Gregory of Nazianzus, taught: "What is not assumed is not redeemed."

Jesus Christ is fully human. This means, contrary to many ancient (and modern) heresies, that he had a human body, mind, will, and soul. Jesus had:

- a body which ate, slept, was tempted and could suffer and die
- a human mind which grew with his human body and which had to grow in wisdom (Luke 2:52)
- a human will, with which he chose to the perfectly do the will of the Father
- a human spirit that descended into Hades.

It is the human nature of Christ who has been exalted to the right hand of the Father, for the divine nature of the Son has always existed in the closest possible union with the Father and the Spirit. In his humanity, Jesus Christ communicates and reveals the divinity of Christ and, therefore, the Holy Trinity.

Why did God become man?

God became man that he might reveal his love to man. The incarnation of Christ and his subsequent ministry were God's ultimate revelation of his love for mankind.

This love of God is expressed in God's desire to *redeem* mankind and restore Man to union with him. Man was the cause of man's death, but God chose to give life through the humanity of Christ (1 Cor 15:21; see also Gal 4:4–5). God became the Second Adam to redeem man from the curse placed upon the first Adam and his heirs. As the writer of Hebrews writes: *"in all things He had to be made like His brethren, that He might be a merciful and faithful High Priest in things pertaining to God, to make propitiation for the sins of the people"* (Heb 2:17).

God became man so that Jesus could perfectly obey the will of the Father for us. Part of the work of redemption, which includes the idea of recapitulation, is for Christ to be the perfect man, into whom we are adopted. Jesus, in his humanity, *chose* to obey the Father, in spite of being fully human and subject to all of the same temptations to which we are subjected. Christ's perfect obedience is shown especially in his offering himself on the cross.

In assuming human nature to redeem it, God revealed his essential goodness. God is, indeed, very good! So good that his nature is always to take evil and transform it into good. In his first miracle at the wedding at Cana, Jesus transformed the utility of water into the joy of wine. But that miracle was tame compared to his perpetual miracle of taking evil and transforming it into good. This grandest of miracles reaches its awe-inspiring zenith in the incarnation and life of Jesus Christ, who took on fallen human nature that he might redeem it.

More unbelievable to many than even the miracle of God's incarnation is his miracle of using suffering as a means of blessing his children immeasurably. But, of course, the miracle of the incarnation and the miracle of God transforming evil into good are, at heart, one and the same.

> *Pour forth, we beseech Thee, O Lord, Thy grace into our hearts; that we, to whom the incarnation of Christ, Thy Son, was made known by the message of an angel, may by His Passion and Cross be brought to the glory of His Resurrection, through the same Christ Our Lord. Amen.* (from the Angelus)

CHAPTER 3

Jesus Took on Human Suffering

Jesus took on not only human nature but also human suffering. It would not be too strong to say that Jesus took on human nature *that* he might take on human suffering, for, ever since the fall, to be human is to suffer. For God to restore man to himself, he needed to redeem man from sin and the consequences of sin, primarily suffering, of which death is only the most ferocious species.

God, therefore, is not outside of our suffering and detached from it but has chosen to inhabit it and share it and all things with us.

God didn't magically take away the sins of the world simply by assuming human nature. The process of atonement required that God transform man *by man*: man, and not God, was the one in need of redemption. And so Jesus Christ, the God-man, took on not only human nature but also human suffering.

To confront and conquer the enemies of God and man—sin and evil, death and the devil—Jesus Christ truly suffered.

We often underestimate suffering, in this case, the suffering of Christ. We've already said that man suffers because of a certain lack of good. In this sense, Christ's suffering began not on Good Friday with his passion but from the time of his incarnation and conception.

Christ came to redeem all mankind from every kind of evil and suffering, and, therefore, he suffered all kinds of evils. This means as well (a point much neglected) that Jesus's sacrifice was not only the six hours on the cross or the twelve or so hours at the passion and crucifixion *but his entire life*. For Jesus's entire life was a giving up of self, a denying of self, and an emptying of self for our good. Every deprivation of the good he deserved was a form of suffering to him.

This is the teaching of Saint Paul in his wondrous hymn in Philippians 2. In explaining Christ's love and humility, Paul speaks of Jesus:

> who, being in the form of God, did not consider it robbery to be equal with God, but made Himself of no reputation, taking the form of a bondservant, and coming in the likeness of men. And being found in appearance as a man, He humbled Himself and became obedient to the point of death, even the death of the cross. (Phil 2:6–9)

Everything that Jesus did as the Christ, he accomplished as the prophesied Suffering Servant: the death of Jesus was prefigured in every moment of the life of Jesus. Jesus, therefore, experienced every genus of human suffering, beginning with his conception, as he recapitulated and redeemed Adam.

JESUS EMPTIED HIMSELF AND TOOK THE FORM OF A MAN

It's difficult to imagine how much God gave up to become man. We all know how humiliating human life is for each of us, who are by nature fallen men. But what of our perfect God, the Creator of the immensities of the universe, who managed to squeeze himself into a form the size of you or me? To take on human nature, God gave himself up, in ways we can't entirely understand. This self-deprivation (all of Jesus's suffering was a voluntary, self-giving suffering) of becoming man is only the first act of suffering in an entire life of self-giving suffering.

JESUS WAS BORN IN HUMILIATING CIRCUMSTANCES

The humiliation of Jesus's birth extended, then, not only to taking on human flesh but also to being born among the beasts. He who was the Bread of Life and who was born in the city of bread was born in a feeding trough for beasts. He who is the only Clean and Holy One was born among the filth of the world. He who is man's true home was born in a homeless condition, and even in birth, the Son of Man had no place to rest his sweet head.

Those swaddling cloths? They were his first shroud, pointing to that death which could not contain life. These humble clothes, Saint Luke says (Luke 2:12), were a *sign*.

JESUS FIRST SHED HIS BLOOD AT HIS CIRCUMCISION

He who is the New Creation on the eighth day, the day of the new creation, shed his blood for us. This was the same blood of the covenant foreshadowed in the old covenant, partaken of in the Lord's Supper, and shed on the cross for the sins of the world.

John Keble, in his poem "The Circumcision of Christ" (from his famous volume *The Christian Year*), wrote:

> The Year begins with Thee,
> And Thou beginn'st with woe,
> To let the world of sinners see
> That blood for sin must flow.
>
> Like sacrificial wine
> Pour'd on a victim's head
> Are those few precious drops of Thine,
> Now first to offering led.
>
> Look here, and hold thy peace:
> The Giver of all good
> Even from the womb takes no release
> From suffering, tears, and blood.

"CAN ANYTHING GOOD COME FROM NAZARETH?"

"Can anything good come from Nazareth?" This was the question Nathanael asked when first hearing about Jesus, and which men have asked ever since. For we mostly assume that bigger is better and that God will come in the more visible and more powerful things of the world.

The King of kings was not only born in humiliating circumstances: He was also raised in them. His entire life was lived in the tiny nation of Israel, chosen by God precisely because she was so weak and small.

He did not grow up in the city of David, where the temple resided, nor was he raised in the more cosmopolitan and "hip" Judea in the south. Instead, he was raised in the obscure town of Nazareth, whose population would only have been a few hundred. So obscure is Nazareth, that although Matthew records that the Holy Family moved to Nazareth "so that what was spoken by the prophets might be fulfilled" (Matt 2:23), there is no direct reference to Nazareth in the Old Testament! It was probably the general humility of Christ's life that fulfilled the Scriptures, rather than Nazareth specifically.

Nazareth was not only obscure but also despised. Nazareth was in the "hick" region of Galilee, itself despised and part of a notorious curse: "Galilean—fool!" It was because of Peter's "hick" accent that those in Jerusalem knew at the time of his denial that he was a Galilean who had been with Jesus. But even the despised Nazareth despised Jesus when he preached his first sermon there. For "they rose up and thrust Him out of the city; and they led Him to the brow of the hill on which their city was built, that they might throw Him down over the cliff" (Luke 4:29).

JESUS LEARNED OBEDIENCE BY WHAT HE SUFFERED

One of the most marvelously mysterious verses in the Holy Scriptures is this: "He learned obedience by the things which He suffered" (Heb 5:8). The terrible obedience of the cross could only have been performed by a life perfectly devoted to the habit of obedience (perhaps in the same way that by a life devoted to fasting and denying self, Jesus prepared himself for the forty days and nights of fasting). Jesus's obedience to his heavenly Father was coordinate with his obedience to his earthly father and mother. Although when Jesus was twelve, he was mature enough to discuss with the teachers of the law in the temple, when he returned home, he was subject to his parents (Luke 2:51).

Jesus came to obey the will of the Father, for he said not only "I have come down from heaven, not to do My own will, but the will of Him who sent Me" (John 6:38) but also "My food is to do the will of Him who sent Me, and to finish His work" (John 4:34). He was without sin, for he perfectly obeyed the will of the Father and perfectly kept the law.

Jesus obeyed the most difficult commandment of all: to take the cup. Although in his humanity, part of him did not desire the cup, his response to the will of the Father was "nevertheless not My will, but Yours, be done" (Luke 22:42).

This obedience was a form of suffering, for it was a giving up of self and its desires and will. All of us who have ever obeyed another, in a matter which we do not desire to, know that obedience involves suffering.

JESUS EXPERIENCED OUR COMMON SUFFERINGS

Often, we focus too exclusively on the extraordinary suffering of Christ: His passion and crucifixion. But these are only the perfection of a life filled with suffering, most of which was "ordinary." Whatever category of suffering we are capable of experiencing, Jesus suffered it for us.

Is any of you weak or tired? Jesus was weak and tired for you. As Gregory Nazianzen said: "And perhaps He goes to sleep, so that He may bless sleep also; perhaps He is tired that He may hallow weariness also; perhaps He weeps that He may make tears blessed" (Oration 37).

Perhaps nothing summarizes the postmodernism condition better than homelessness. For while more people live in homes that they own than ever before (and larger ones at that), we are lost in the cosmos, without a place or identity, and far from our true home. Is any of you homeless or hungry? Jesus fasted and went without meals for you. The Maker of Homes, the Home of homes, our Eternal Home, went homeless for you.

Is any of you poor? Jesus emptied himself for you. He gave up the certainty and security of his trade and relied on the gifts of others for three years. Having created everything, he owned nothing.

Has any of you endured mocking, spitting, hitting, and scourging? In spite of the fact that we have each done these things to Christ, he has borne them all for us.

Has any of you been betrayed or abandoned? The postmodern condition of homelessness is caused, in large part, by our betraying and abandoning one another. We live in a culture of divorce, for we divide that which God has joined. We do this not only in the holy bonds of matrimony but also in every possible human relationship. We break up, withdraw, move away from home, and distance ourselves from one another. Although we betrayed and abandoned Jesus, he took betrayal and abandonment from us and made them his own.

We might expect this from our enemies or opponents, but it always hurts most when we are betrayed or abandoned by those we love and who have loved us. Husbands and wives, parents and children, brothers and sisters, friends and friends, pastors and parishioners: our own familiar friends betray us, and it hurts like hell because it is truly a taste of that abandoned and divorced and homeless place.

Has any of you been tried or condemned unjustly? Here, we find ourselves standing in awe at the epicenter of God's catastrophic deliverance. For throughout his life, and especially at his trial and on the cross, Jesus was tried and condemned—*for you*. At the cross, the only perfect and just man to live was condemned by sinful men. This condemnation was catholic in scope, for who was to blame for putting Jesus to death? Both Jew and gentile, both you and me, and us and them.

Not only did the Just die for the unjust (1 Pet 3:18): the *Judge* died for the guilty. It isn't only that a just man died for another just man, and it's even more than the Just Man dying for unjust men. On the cross, the sentence of the divine Judge was taken up by the Judge himself. This is the Good News: that God put himself in our place that he might put us in his place.

THE SUFFERING OF THE CROSS

Jesus died an excruciating death for you. He experienced and triumphed over every kind of pain. We often meditate on the immense physical pain He experienced for us, and much has been written from a medical standpoint of exactly how he suffered. Great was this pain indeed!

But his physical pain was neither his only nor his greatest pain. As Christ approached the cross, his sufferings multiplied exponentially. He wept over Jerusalem and the temple because Israel would not repent: the bride had left the bridegroom at the altar, and a divorce was in process. He was rejected by his own people, especially the rulers, teachers, and leaders.

Even more hurtful was the rejection of Jesus by his own familiar friends. Judas betrayed him; Peter denied him three times; and all of the disciples forsook him and fled. Any of us who have had family members or close friends turn on us or reject us know in part the pain of Jesus.

He was treated unfairly and judged unjustly by the whole world, both gentile and Jew. Any of us who have been treated unfairly know a little of Jesus's misery.

He was mocked by both Jew and gentile, spat upon, hit in the face, and scourged to within an inch of his life. The suffering of all of these things was more than a physical pain: it was a humiliation of his whole person.

Jesus's chief suffering was in bearing the sins of the world and the punishment for them. So great was this suffering that even the anticipation of it caused Christ such great agony that his sweat became like great drops of blood falling down to the ground (Luke 22:44).

The death of Jesus on a cross is of special importance. For the Romans, crucifixion was a symbol and device of torture and punishment. It demonstrated not only the sinfulness of men who deserved to die but also the sinfulness of those who delighted in such cruelty. For us, it symbolizes not only the justice in the death penalty we all have deserved but also the injustice of sinful men putting the sinless Christ to death. It is also a means of humiliation, since the one being crucified is exposed and naked and subject to many humiliations as a result.

Christ endured the curse of the cross for you and me. The cross is a kind of tree, and the Scriptures teach: "he who is hanged is accursed of God" (Deut 21:23; Gal 3:13). Adam's disobedience concerned a tree, resulting in death. Christ's obedience concerned a tree, resulting in death for Christ but life for man. The instrument of death devised and deserved by man has become the Tree of Life for those in union with Christ.

You and I cannot possibly imagine the suffering involved in taking on the sins of the world. All we can imagine is the worst pain and suffering we have experienced and extrapolate from it. But Christ paid the price for the sins of the world; he suffered the penalty and punishment due to man in his entirety.

He who is the Lord and Giver of Life truly died, and the Word which created all things fell silent. Jesus did mortal combat with death and conquered it for us all. His death, and all human deaths, is the ultimate suffering because the good of which we are deprived is life itself. Every human who has ever been touched by death knows how painful it is.

THE CUP WHICH JESUS TOOK

Christ took the cup of suffering for us.

He endured and took upon himself *all* human suffering and suffered and died to redeem every bit of human suffering. The Father prepared for him a table in the midst of his enemies, and he drank the cup of human suffering that the Father commanded him to drink.

This cup is many mysterious things. It is, in fact, all of the suffering and evil the world has ever known. In the movie *Time Bandits*, there's a scene in which a fifty-five-gallon drum filled with Concentrated Evil is, unfortunately, spilled. Evil doesn't really work like that: it's not a substance but a parasitical mutator and destroyer of Good. But the cup which Christ drank on the cross was, perhaps, concentrated evil after all. For on the cross, Christ consumed all of the suffering and evil the world has known or ever will know.

Every form of evil and suffering, by which good is destroyed or denied us, was present in the cup. Every suffering that is the result of rejecting God and his goodness, and every sin that will ever be committed, was dissolved into that cup. In it were all of the sins, injustices, hatred, and wrongs of the world.

And yet, Christ chose to drink it for us.

While the fullness of suffering and evil was present in the cup of the Cross, Jesus's entire life was cruciform. All of his life, as we have said earlier, was suffering.

Jesus's entire life was a drinking of the cup.

Jesus's entire life was an appropriation of the suffering and evil of the world.

Jesus's entire life was a sacrificial offering of God, of man, of self, to God.

The truth is: *Christ was sipping on the cup of suffering for thirty-three years, but at Calvary he drained the cup, dregs and all.*

This was that cup, promised and prophesied in the old covenant and fulfilled in the new. Here is the cup, promised to the world as a righteous judgment for our sins. God gives this cup to all the wicked: "For in the hand of the Lord there is a cup, and the wine is red; it is fully mixed, and He pours it out; surely its dregs shall all the wicked of the earth drain and drink down" (Ps 75:8).

The cup is given as well to Israel: "Awake, awake! Stand up, O Jerusalem, you who have drunk at the hand of the Lord the cup of His fury; you have drunk the dregs of the cup of trembling, and drained it out" (Isa 51:17).

The Lord promised the cup to all nations, without exception, for their sins (Jer 25:15–28).

It is not surprising that sinful men and nations must drink the cup of suffering for their sins. The wonder of the salvation is this: that God himself quaffed the cup for us. The righteous judgment of the Righteous Judge was swallowed by God himself. He made that cup of eternal poison and Concentrated Evil that should have been ours his instead.

But when the Father said, "No, you must drink," the Son said, "Yes, Father, I will."

The Second Cup, Part I

After the Last Supper, Jesus took the cup, blessed it, and gave it to his disciples. This was probably the third cup, the cup of blessing. But Jesus does not yet take the final cup at the Passover. For Jesus "took the cup, and gave thanks, and said, "Take this and divide it among yourselves; for I say to you, I will not drink of the fruit of the vine until the kingdom of God comes'" (Luke 22:17–18).

Jesus has temporarily postponed drinking and sharing the final cup. But when do we see the cup next appear in the Gospels? In the Garden of Gethsemane, where the Father offers Jesus the cup, and Jesus prays for the Father to take it from him.

Jesus prayed: "Father, if it is Your will, take this cup away from Me; nevertheless not My will, but Yours, be done" (Luke 22:42).

Here is the final cup: here is the completion of the New Passover and the coming of the kingdom in all of its power and glory.

The obedience of the first Adam was relatively easy: be fruitful and multiply (know your wife and bear children, among other things); take dominion over the earth (every man's dream); and eat from the fruit of every tree but one (a paradisaical buffet, with one dish off-limits). But the obedience of the Second Adam was exceedingly difficult: take upon yourself the sins and suffering of the world; bear the judgment of God against man; give of yourself until you die.

All human wrestling, against God, self, neighbor, and creation, was present in the garden. But while we too often recapitulate the fall and its mortal "No," Jesus said "Yes" out of love. "All you need is love" turns out to be true, but not in the way the Beatles or others have imagined. For out of love, God created the world, and out of love, he redeemed it. But this love required the Father to give his only-begotten Son to die for the world; this love required the Son to give up his life as a ransom for man; and this love required the Spirit to bind God not only to himself but now to man and his suffering.

This transfiguring, transmogrifying love transforms suffering into sacrifice. For Jesus was not a passive bearer of the sins and suffering of the world: out of love, he *chose* them for himself.

At first, Jesus refused the wine when it was offered. But in the end, he drank the cup for you and for me:

> After this, Jesus, knowing that all things were now accomplished, that the Scripture might be fulfilled, said, 'I thirst!' Now a vessel full of sour wine was sitting there; and they filled a sponge with sour wine, put it on hyssop, and put it to His mouth. So when Jesus

had received the sour wine, He said, 'It is finished!' And bowing His head, He gave up His spirit" (John 19:28–29).

Just as Jesus prepared a table for his disciples (including Judas) at the Last Supper, so the Father prepared a table for Jesus in the presence of his enemies. Adam and Eve betrayed God at the First Supper, eating the food prescribed by the Serpent while fasting from obedience to God. In the garden of God, man first betrayed God.

Again, at the Last Supper, a man betrayed Jesus, for the serpent, retreating after Christ's victory in the wilderness, returned at the Supper and then the garden. After Judas had taken the bread from Christ, Satan entered into him (John 13:27), and Judas left the Supper. While Christ's Supper is a means of life to those who faithfully partake, Judas was at this moment excommunicated and barred from the table.

In the garden of Gethsemane, Jesus was tempted again, as he was in the wilderness, to refuse the will of the Father and to follow his own human will. But in this garden, man said the difficult "Yes," and love began to conquer the world.

Jesus Christ took the cup for you and for me. He took on not only human nature but also all human suffering, and this has made possible the redemption of humanity and the transformation of suffering into a means of glory and joy.

> *Ah, holy Jesus, how hast thou offended,*
> *that we to judge thee have in hate pretended?*
> *By foes derided, by thine own rejected,*
> *O most afflicted!*
>
> *Who was the guilty? Who brought this upon thee?*
> *Alas, my treason, Jesus, hath undone thee!*
> *'Twas I, Lord Jesus, I it was denied thee;*
> *I crucified thee.*
>
> *Lo, the Good Shepherd for the sheep is offered;*
> *the slave hath sinned, and the Son hath suffered.*
> *For our atonement, while we nothing heeded,*
> *God interceded.*
>
> *For me, kind Jesus, was thy incarnation,*
> *thy mortal sorrow, and thy life's oblation;*
> *thy death of anguish and thy bitter passion,*
> *for my salvation.*

The Second Cup, Part I

Therefore, kind Jesus, since I cannot pay thee,
I do adore thee, and will ever pray thee,
think on thy pity and thy love unswerving,
not my deserving.
(Johann Heermann, translated by Robert Bridges)

CHAPTER 4

Jesus Has Transformed the Meaning of Suffering

THE GREAT TRANSMUTATION

When Christ consumed the cup of suffering, he transfigured the world forever.

When Christ consumed the cup, he transformed the meaning of suffering.

When Christ consumed the cup, he transmuted its contents from evil into good.

God's judgment upon man was translated from "guilty!" to "not guilty."

Death was transported into life.

Suffering was transmogrified from punishment and a sign of death and judgment into glory and joy and a sign that God is with us.

God is famous for performing miracles: we read of Jesus turning water into wine, healing lepers and the lame from their infirmities, and raising people from the dead. God himself is a living miracle. First, is the miracle of the Holy Trinity, three persons, and one God. Then, comes the miracle of Christ, who is forever both God and man. Even man is a miracle, having been created *ex nihilo* by God in the beginning.

Aside from the miracle that is God himself, God's greatest miracle is transforming evil into good.

The Second Cup, Part I

For Jesus Christ is the True Alchemist. You might remember that medieval alchemists endeavored to transmute base elements such as lead and mercury into the nobler elements of gold and silver. While the alchemical Philosopher's Stone was never discovered (which could not only transmute elements but would also transmute men into immortals), the Theologian's Stone has been present to all since the first century. We need no hermetical religion, for the Great Transmutation wrought by Christ is open and visible to all.

To help us comprehend such an incomprehensibility as the transformation of evil into good, I will begin with a question: "Was the cross of Jesus a good or evil thing?"

The twentieth and twenty-first centuries have reminded us all of the great evil of which man is capable, one of the worst of which is the taking of the life of another made in the image of God. Worse still would be to be a mass murderer, especially on the grand scale of Mao, Stalin, or Hitler.

But undoubtedly the worst thing men could ever imagine or do, the very thing they did, was to murder the King of Glory. Was the crucifixion of Christ, therefore, a good or an evil thing? Both. It was meant for evil in the hands of sinful men but meant for good by God.

Jesus is the new Joseph (as well as the New Adam, New Abel, New Noah, New Moses, New Joshua, and New David). Out of envy and hatred, Joseph's brothers sold him into slavery. But, due to God's love and providence, Joseph not only prospered personally: he also saved the world, especially Israel. The climax of Joseph's story, when he is reunited with his brothers, comes when he says to them: "But as for you, you meant evil against me; but God meant it for good, in order to bring it about as it is this day, to save many people alive" (Gen 50:20).

What men and Satan mean for evil, God means for good. This is true not only for Joseph but also for the Christian and all Christian suffering.

And what does this cross lead to for the human nature of Christ? Saint Paul says that Christ "humbled Himself and became obedient to the point of death, even the death of the cross. Therefore God also has highly exalted Him and given Him the name which is above every name, that at the name of Jesus every knee should bow" (Phil 2:8–10).

Because the Son obediently offered himself as a sacrifice for the sins and suffering of mankind, God the Father exalted him to glory. By his suffering and death, the Suffering Servant has established his everlasting kingdom and dethroned the usurpers—sin, death, and Satan. What Satan meant as a way of humiliating and harming Christ, the Father meant as a way of glorifying Christ and exalting his human nature to his right hand, where glory and joy abound forevermore.

By his suffering, Jesus has transformed *all* Christian suffering, experienced with and for him. What was once the just punishment for sin, and the necessary consequence for disobeying God and disordering his creation and our hearts, is now the means of union with Christ. What was once merely pain and suffering has now become a means to glory and joy in Christ.

Make no mistake: suffering is not inherently redemptive but is instead inherently evil and destructive. But suffering is both redeemable and a means of redemption because the Redeemer suffered for us and unites himself to us by his suffering. When we are united to the suffering of Christ, suffering becomes a means of union with Christ. And Jesus Christ is the source not only of our eternal glory but also our present joy.

Behold how mighty our Crucified, Resurrected, and Ascended Lord is!

Everything King Midas touched turned to gold, and it became for him a curse. But everything God touches turns to good, and it becomes for us the source of all blessing. Everything he touches becomes converted to him or dies, and whatever remains is a sacrament of his presence and a means of union with him.

Christ has sanctified suffering, even the ultimate suffering of death. He has experienced it and hallowed it, and whatever touches him becomes holy. Suffering is now a means of union with him.

Even death is mocked, for it has been tamed and made a door to life. Christ is so powerful that when he touches death, death dies; when he touches sin, sin flees and evaporates; and when he touches suffering, he unites himself to us.

Suffering itself is still evil by nature but bows before him and serves him by blessing us as a means of union with Christ. God transforms and redeems even the evil of suffering into good! He mutates death into life, suffering into joy, and humiliation into glory. This is why he and we suffer.

This is what we call "salvation," and it is glorious and grand, for it is the taking away of all evil and suffering and turning them into good.

The very meaning of suffering is, therefore, transformed for the Christian united to Christ.

The Second Cup, Part I

Far from being a sign of God's nonexistence, apathy, or impotence, human suffering is transformed by Christ's incarnation into a sacrament of God's presence, love, and power.

The cross is the symbol of this great transformation.

Haven't you ever thought it a little weird that these Christians go around wearing miniature torture devices around their necks? Why would we do this? Because we see in the cross, that symbol of both Christ's suffering *and ours*, not death but life. The cross, that Roman death device planted in the garden, turns out to be the Tree of Life.

In the old creation, the first Adam sinned in the garden and ate of a tree which led to death. In the new creation, in the New Garden, there lay a tree and a tomb as well. But in this new creation, the Second Adam was tested and obeyed. The tree was the Tree of Death, the cross, upon which the Second Adam hung for your sins. But Christ has transfigured this Tree of Death to become for us the Tree of Life.

And that tomb? Well, the tomb was planted in the middle of a garden. For we read in John 19:41, "now in the place where He was crucified there was a Garden, and in the garden a new tomb, wherein no man had yet been laid." It is a new tomb because it is the tomb in which the Son of God was placed. It is a new tomb because it is a tomb that cannot hold its occupant.

But there is another body placed into that tomb, after Christ has left it empty. For Christ has escaped the tomb, and in the tomb he has placed the corpse of death itself, for Christ puts death to death. The tomb is sin's, death's, and the devil's, but the garden is now ours again.

Why does Mary suppose, in verse 15 of chapter 20, that Jesus is the gardener? Because he is the Second Adam, placed in the garden to keep it, since the first Adam would not.

The presence of the angels at the tomb in the garden alerts us to the fact that we have witnessed the New Creation. Just as angels were present at the annunciation and birth of Christ, they also attend the birth of the New Creation at the resurrection. They are the cherubim that God commissioned to keep the first Adam out of the garden. But these same cherubim are the ones who now herald the entrance of the Second Adam into the garden, and they escort him in.

They are the cherubim who are placed on both ends of the mercy seat, the place of God's special presence in glory, in the holy of holies in the temple. And Christ has become the new temple, for those angels are placed at his head and his feet in the tomb that now stands open to man.

In drinking the cup for us, Jesus has made all things new. He has transformed evil into good; death into life; humiliation into glory; sorrow into joy; the cross into a Tree of Life; and suffering into a means of union with him.

The thesis of the book and the gospel of suffering proclaim this truth: that if we suffer first with Christ, we shall also be raised to glory and joy with him. All of the Scriptures proclaim this most liberating and welcome of truths. As Jesus taught (from the Old Testament) his disciples on the road to Emmaus: "Ought not the Christ to have suffered these things and to enter into His glory?" (Luke 24:26).

THE CROSS IS THE GLORY OF CHRIST

We Christians wear crosses and crucifixes around our necks and put them as the focal point of our tables and altars because the cross is the means of our salvation and is the glory of Jesus Christ, our Lord. The cross is the glory of Christ because it is the ultimate revelation of the goodness, power, and love of God, which together constitute his glory.

The cross is the glory of Christ not only because of the glorious salvation he has brought to men but also because it is the means by which he is lifted up, exalted, and glorified. Now when we say that Jesus has been glorified in the crucifixion and resurrection, we mean, primarily, his human nature, for the divine nature of Christ never left the Father's throne. It is the *human* nature of Christ that is glorified (and, as we'll see later, this means the potential for our human nature to be glorified with him.)

This glory of the cross, of course, included much suffering in this life for Jesus.

Jesus was glorified by the Father precisely because of his death for us on the cross. The writer of Hebrews tells us that Jesus was crowned with glory and honor because of the suffering of death" (Heb 2:9; see also Phil 2:8–10).

Although to human eyes the cross was Christ's despised and shameful emptying of himself and his humiliation, in the eyes of the Father, it was the glorification of the Son. For on the cross, Jesus fulfilled his human destiny and perfectly obeyed the will of the Father. As he himself so often preached: the last became first, and the least became the greatest.

Therefore, the King of kings, God Almighty in persons, *is* the Suffering Servant, and the cross is his throne!

God's kingdom, Jesus reveals to us, is perpetually shown by his humiliation and suffering. On the one hand, suffering and humiliation are the means to a future and greater glory and joy. On the other hand, suffering and humiliation are also how we see and experience the glory and joy of the Lord, even now.

Consider our King!

Matthew's Gospel portrays Jesus as the promised Messiah and the king of the Jews, but this King was born in humility. This King was born in humble circumstances: the feeding trough in the stable described in Luke 2. The wise men came all the way from the East to seek and worship Jesus as the king of the Jews when he was an infant or toddler (Matthew 2:2). Herod knew this helpless infant to be the king of the Jews, and, therefore, out of jealousy and hatred, plotted his Satanic murder.

On Palm Sunday, the crowds sang royal hymns to Jesus, proclaiming him to be the Messiah or king: "Hosanna to the Son of David!" (Matt 21:9). The city which Christ was entering was the royal city of David, Jerusalem. However, the way he entered indicated the way in which his kingdom was coming:

> Tell the daughter of Zion,
> 'Behold, your King is coming to you,
> Lowly, and sitting on a donkey,
> A colt, the foal of a donkey.' (Matt 21:5, quoting Zech 9:9)

Christ's rule as King and the coming of his kingdom were far different than what the Jews expected. The Messiah prophesied so often in the Old Testament turned out to be the Suffering Servant of Isaiah 53 and Psalm 22, which is fulfilled in incredible detail by the crucifixion of Christ. The Suffering-Servant vocation and the royal vocation are one in Christ.

Throughout his trial and passion, in the midst of his humiliation, Jesus was revealed to be the king of Israel. When asked by Pilate if he were the king of the Jews, Jesus answered: "It is as you say" (v. 11). The soldiers mockingly acknowledged Christ's kingship, bowing the knee and saying "Hail, King of the Jews!" (v. 29). The leaders of the Jews mocked his kingship as well, saying: "If He is the King of Israel, let Him now come down from the cross, and we will believe Him" (v. 42).

The climax of Christ's revelation as the Suffering Servant who is also King was his crucifixion. It was even while he hung on the cross that all could read that he was the "King of the Jews." It was at the point of Christ's death that the Roman centurion recognized him as the Son of God. Jesus himself taught that "When you lift up the Son of Man, then you will know that I am He" (John 8:28).

Christ was enthroned on the cross, for it was by the cross that his kingdom came and by the cross that he defeated the kingdom of Satan. His crown, therefore, was not a crown of precious jewels but a crown of thorns. It was not his disciples who were with him on his right and left hand but criminals and sinners, like us.

The fact that Christ's kingdom came through the cross, and continues to come through the cross, is illustrated by the ways in which Christ's crucifixion pictures what Jesus taught about his kingdom in the Sermon on the Mount in Matthew 5. Jesus taught that the kingdom of heaven belonged to those who were poor in spirit (Matt 5:3), as Christ was, especially in his death. He taught his disciples that "Blessed are those who are persecuted for righteousness' sake, for theirs is the kingdom of heaven" (Matt 5:10), and no one was more persecuted than Jesus himself.

And so the cross of Christ is the glory of Christ because by it he is revealed to be the king. The cross, therefore, is also Christ's scepter by which he rules the world by serving it.

The cross, Jesus says (and we must say with him), is also his hour of glory. Right after the Triumphal Entry, Jesus preaches: "The hour has come that the Son of Man should be glorified" (John 12:23). Jesus continues by revealing: "'Now My soul is troubled, and what shall I say? "Father, save Me from this hour"? But for this purpose I came to this hour. Father, glorify Your name.' Then a voice came from heaven, saying, 'I have both glorified it and will glorify it again'" (John 12:27–28).

Here, at the cross, the Tree of Life where the great reversal took place, Christ's glory is seen by his suffering.

By his suffering and death, Christ has defanged and killed death: by his suffering and death, Christ has transfigured death into the portal to life everlasting.

By his suffering and death, Christ has forever transformed the cruelest and most humiliating symbol of suffering and death, the cross, into the supreme Christian symbol of hope, love, and life.

By his suffering and death, Christ has exchanged humiliation for glory and sorrow for joy.

By his suffering and death, Christ has rewritten the tragic story of humanity so that it is now a comedy.

THE SECOND CUP, PART I

THE CROSS AND THE RESURRECTION ARE A SINGLE SAVING EVENT

Where is the resurrection in all of this? By choosing to focus on suffering, my heart most naturally meditates on the meaning of the cross. But Jesus's suffering on the cross and his glory in his resurrection are *inseparable*. It's not just that they're related chronologically as cause and effect: they are *perichoretic*, that is, they both partake of each other. They are, in fact, the two edges of the sword of God's self-revelation.

Both the cross and the resurrection are historical and trans-historical events which God enacts, out of love, on behalf of humanity. Although the cross stands for everything to which God is opposed, God became the cross for us. But in becoming the cross, in taking on all human suffering and incarnating himself in it, God utterly and eternally transformed it, as we have said.

God's glory is shown, therefore, not only in the resurrection, but also in the cross, and especially in the cross and resurrection together. While the cross is Christ's taking on the sins and suffering of the world, the resurrection is the demonstration of his victory over his enemies and ours. The resurrection is the Father's justification of Christ, in his ministry and in his sacrifice, and, therefore, of us in Christ.

There can be no resurrection without the cross and no cross without the resurrection. This means that even in the joyful, glorious celebration of Christ's resurrection in the Eucharist, we are also celebrating, proclaiming, and partaking of Christ's cross. On a practical note, this means that we might sorrow and suffer, even in the Eucharist, as we take the cup of Christ. Although Christ's mighty work is finished, we still partake of the cross.

But the union of cross and resurrection also means that even in the humiliating and painful suffering of this world, we are conquerors with Christ, partakers of his resurrection and ascension, and stand in his blessed presence where we discover joy and glory!

> *Grant, O Lord, that as we are baptized into the death of thy blessed Son our Saviour Jesus Christ, so by continually mortifying our corrupt affections we may be buried with him; and that, through the grave, and gate of death, we may pass to our joyful resurrection; for his merits, who died, and was buried, and rose again for us, thy Son Jesus Christ our Lord. Amen.*
> (Collect for Easter Even, 1928 *Book of Common Prayer*)

CHAPTER 5

Suffering Is How We See God

All that we have been saying so far yields a most joyful and peaceable fruit: *that suffering is how we see God*. This epiphany, counterintuitive and even offensive as it may seem, turns out to be at the center of the good news about God.

In the last chapter, I concluded by saying that the cross is the glory of Christ. This is only another way of saying that suffering is how God reveals himself to us. For glory is the visible, brilliant manifestation of the essential goodness and beauty of God.

All men seek a vision of God. Christians call the state of bliss for which we hope the Beatific Vision of God. Even in this life, God promises to his children that they may see him. But the way he chooses to reveal himself to us in this life frequently involves suffering.

The cross of Jesus, the sum and symbol of all human suffering, is the glory of God.

The cross of Jesus is the way we see God.

The cross of Jesus is the means by which the kingdom of God enters into human history.

It is the sign, symbol, and sacrament of God's love for man.

And, therefore, the cross of Jesus is the path to our glory and joy.

We recognize Jesus Christ by the suffering he shows us: the hole in his side and the wounds in his hands. Jesus invites us—if we will see him and follow him—to partake of his sufferings with all of our senses and all of our bodies and souls. He encourages us to place our bodies in his body, our hands in his hands, and our hands in his side, from which his body and bride are born. Our life is hidden in Christ, which means his pierced but resurrected body.

Perhaps his wounds exist to let us in.

When Jesus revealed himself to his disciples in the Upper Room, after the resurrection, he revealed himself by showing them his scarred hands and the wound in his side. Why would he do this? He was showing them the love of God—he was showing them the kingdom of God. He was saying that by these signs he would forever after be known.

And this is why, as we will see later, Jesus is always known to his disciples in the breaking of the bread and the taking of the cup. For by these we proclaim and partake of Christ's death and resurrection until his coming again.

Whenever we meet with Jesus in his Upper Room to see his battle-scarred hands, he comes with forgiveness in his holy hands. He raises his hands in benediction and says "Peace" to his disciples.

For *the Price of Peace is the Prince of Peace.*

Not only do we recognize Jesus by his wounds: we also see ourselves in them. For the Good Shepherd brands his sheep and calls them all by name by sharing his wounds with them and marking them out by the death and resurrection of baptism.

If you want to see God, then behold the crucified, risen Jesus Christ!

Jesus says: "When I have been lifted up, then you will know that I AM!" (John 8:28.) Let that settle in a moment.

Jesus means: "When I have been lifted up on the Cross and crucified, I will be glorified, and you will know that I AM, the God of Abraham, Isaac, and Jacob and the Maker of heaven and earth."

Philip said to Jesus, "Lord, show us the Father, and it is sufficient for us." Jesus said to him, "Have I been with you so long, and yet you have not known Me, Philip? He who has seen Me has seen the Father" (John 14:9). And so when we see the Suffering Servant, we are seeing the face of God, the glory of the invisible God made visible in the anguished visage of Christ, the Son.

It is this Christ, the crucified, resurrected Christ, with his wounded hands and side, who is the image of the invisible God (Col 1:15).

The universal experience of humanity, including Christians, is that they fail to see God very well or very often. Could this be because we are looking for him in the wrong places?

What if a primary way we see God is in suffering?

What if this is the message of the cross, the same cross that Peter at first rejected?

What if the reason we don't see God is that we are primarily looking for the Christ of the miracles and the transfiguration, but it is usually the Christ of the passion that shows up?

What if we are looking for the Lion of Judah or Aslan, but instead Christ comes to us, riding lowly on a donkey, and as the Lamb being led to the slaughter?

The cross, we must remember, is on the top of God's holy mountain. The cross is where God meets man in his suffering, because that is where man now resides. As we said, when we discussed Christ's suffering, his incarnation is into a life of suffering, from conception until death.

It's in the darkness of the cross that Christ is seen to be the Light of the World.

We miss God because we will not take up the cross. Refusing the cup of suffering, we find it hard to see the Christ whose cross has been united to our own.

The cross of Jesus takes the shape of all of our individual and diverse crosses, of every single one of our sufferings, deprivations, and humiliations. When we will see Jesus only in his glory and not his cross, we will not see him much, if at all. When we see him even his cross, but only look to the single moment of Calvary, we will also miss the frequent, indeed perpetual, times he comes to us every day in our own suffering and the suffering of those we love.

And when I demand to see God only when things go my way, I am no better than the Jews, who kept seeking physical healing and miracles from Jesus, when what He was truly offering was forgiveness of sins and union with him.

God is hidden in plain sight in our suffering.

The Father's love has a form, and that form is Jesus Christ, the Son. The Son's love has a shape, and its shape is that of the Cross.

For the Christian, therefore, suffering is never just suffering: it is a means to see God, and soon we'll see how it is also a means of partaking of God's nature.

The sign of the cross is also the sign of the Trinity, and not just that of the Son. For the whole of God—the Father, the Son, and the Holy Spirit—gives himself to us in suffering. It's no accident that the priest or pastor marks us with a cross when he baptizes us into the Name of the Father, and of the Son, and of the Holy Spirit.

It shouldn't surprise us that suffering is a sign of the presence of God. Shouldn't we be somewhat suspicious of a God who claimed to be eternal, all-powerful, and all-wise, and yet acted just like we'd expect him to? The world's religions are filled with just such gods.

But the God who claims to be the God of gods, the God of the Bible, is very strange. This is exactly how it should be. And so the last shall be first and the first last; if you exalt yourself, God will humiliate you; and if you humble yourself, God will exalt you. Suffering, therefore, is both a way God reveals himself and the way we receive him.

Although I've been emphasizing the cross of Christ, this presence of God is seen not by the cross alone but the cross in the context of the resurrection. It is the hands of the crucified *and risen* Lord that are raised for us to see. It is the side of the crucified *and risen* Lord into which we must enter if we would enter into life. To grasp Jesus's presence among us, we must touch his wounds in the context of his resurrection, just like Thomas, with whom we then say, "My Lord and my God!"

If, therefore, you can see God in both poverty and plenty, in suffering and satiety, you will always see God.

Far from being a sign and symbol of God's non-existence, apathy, or impotence, human suffering is transformed by Christ's incarnation into a sacrament of God's presence, love, and power. And by suffering, first Christ's and then ours, we shall see God!

> *Humbly I adore thee, Verity unseen,*
> *who thy glory hidest, 'neath these shadows mean;*
> *lo, to thee surrendered, my whole heart is bowed,*
> *tranced as it beholds thee, shrined within the cloud.*
>
> *Taste and touch and vision to discern thee fail;*
> *faith, that comes by hearing, pierces through the veil.*
> *I believe whate'er the Son of God hath told;*
> *what the Truth hath spoken, that for truth I hold.*
>
> *O memorial wondrous of the Lord's own death;*
> *living Bread that givest all they creatures breath,*
> *grant my spirit ever by thy life may live,*
> *to my taste thy sweetness never failing give.*

Jesus, whom now hidden, I by faith behold,
what my soul doth long for, that thy word foretold;
face to face thy splendor, I at last shall see,
in the glorious vision, blessed Lord, of thee. (Thomas Aquinas)

THE SECOND CUP, PART II

Union with Christ by Suffering

CHAPTER 1

Christ Shares His Human Nature with the Church

So far, we have seen how suffering is not a sign of God's absence, apathy, or impotence but is instead a sign of his presence, love, and power and glory. This is the Christian faith: that God became man that he might suffer for us to remove our suffering and its root cause, sin.

As wondrous as this revelation is, we now process to a truth that is its equal in wonder and power: *because Christ has become man and suffered to redeem man, suffering is a primary means of participating in God's nature and being united to him.*

Everything we've been saying about God suffering for man to reveal himself as a God of love who redeems man is true. But something's missing from the story. It's not yet clear how Jesus dying on the cross has anything to do with us. How is *Christ's* suffering translated into *our* glory and joy?

God's presence, power, and love would not be given to man by Christ's life unless, by some means, the life of Christ, including his suffering, was communicated to his people. This, therefore, is the extraordinary significance of the incarnation: that the divine and human natures are united in Christ. That fellowship of love which the Father, the Son, and the Spirit have always had is now communicable to man.

This blessed union with God, for which man was created and redeemed out of love, is possible only for those who are united to Jesus Christ, the suffering incarnated God.

The Second Cup, Part II

From the beginning, God, who is love, intended to give the best gift and do the greatest good for man, and this greatest of gifts and blessings was himself. And so throughout the Bible, God's relationship with man is portrayed as a marriage between God and man. The Bible begins and ends with a wedding, in what has been called "nuptial bookends."[1] In the beginning, man married woman. But in the end, God marries man, as Jesus, the holy bridegroom, marries his bride at the Marriage Feast of the Lamb (Rev 19:6–10; 21:2–3).

The crux of understanding human suffering is that God has united himself to mankind, including his suffering. So closely has God come to man that Saint Peter teaches that we have become partakers of the divine nature (2 Pet 2:14). By partaking of the divine nature, as we shall see, we partake of the sufferings, the death, the life, and the glory of Christ and, therefore, of God.

It's essential to understand that the things we proclaim about Christ that happen in the Creed are things that happen especially to him in his human nature, which he shares with his church. It is the human Christ who was born of Mary, suffered, died, resurrected, and ascended to the right hand of the Father.

This new, "divinized," human nature, which is Christ's, is shared with the church, who partakes of Christ and has a blessed union with him. For this reason, the church is called the body of Christ, for Christ is truly in us through his Spirit. We have become "one flesh" with Christ so that we are not only the body of Christ but also his holy bride.

An excellent place to apprehend these truths is the first two chapters of the Acts of the Apostles. The beginning of the book of Acts is an underappreciated portion of Scripture. For while much attention has been focused on the miraculous outpouring of the Spirit on the Day of Pentecost, too much of this attention has been on the miracle of Pentecost and not the larger context of the entire story of the Bible and God's unfolding story of redemption. The miracle of Pentecost is only a sign of something much more miraculous, even if less visible and tangible.

What Acts 1–2 teaches us is a profound lesson in the deeper meaning of the incarnation, the ascension, and the church as the mystical body of Christ.

The great message of Luke's Acts of the Apostles is to reveal the *rest* of what Jesus Christ is teaching and doing, which he is doing through his

---

1. West, *Theology of the Body Explained*, 15.

mystical body, the church: "In the first book, O Theophilus, I have dealt with all that Jesus *began* to do and teach" (Acts 1:1).

Luke implies that his second book (Acts) is about the *rest* of what Jesus *began* to do and teach in Luke's first book (the Gospel of Luke). After Christ's human nature ascended into heaven in Acts 1, Jesus sends his Holy Spirit into his body, so that the church becomes the living body of Christ on earth.[2] Throughout the book of Acts, therefore, the church teaches and does what Jesus taught and did: how could it be otherwise, since what they are doing is really what Jesus is doing through them?

And so the apostles heal a lame man, raise people from the dead, and preach the resurrected Christ. They encounter resistance both from Jews and gentiles and are tried unjustly. When Stephen, the first Christian martyr, dies, he dies as Christ, asking that the Father forgive his murderers, for they know not what they do (Acts 7:60).

When, therefore, the church in the book of Acts and the church today (for the church is one) suffer, they suffer *as* Jesus Christ. The language Jesus uses when he calls Saint Paul on the road to Damascus is striking: "Saul, Saul, why are you persecuting *Me*?" (Acts 9:4, italics added). So closely does Jesus identify with his body and bride, the church, that even though Saul is persecuting *the church*, Jesus asks Saul why he's persecuting *him*.

As the body of Christ, we are united to the whole Christ, and this involves his suffering because the life of Christ to which we are united was a life of suffering for and with us. The church, as the body of Christ and in union with Christ, suffers for, with, and *as* Jesus Christ.

As John Keble taught, the church is the extension of Christ's incarnation. It is the locus of God's divine activity among men today. To say that the church is the body of Christ is no mere metaphor but a metaphysical reality whose significance we are scarcely able to and scarcely dare to imagine.

And yet this is *the* message of the Bible: that God became man. This New Man is not merely an individual human person but a new human nature in Christ, which is shared with all who have been united to Christ by baptism and faith.

The first two chapters of Acts also define for us true Christian spirituality. *Christian spirituality is the life of Christ communicated to the body of Christ by the Spirit of Christ.* Only if we first grasp this redemptive truth will

---

2. Pentecost is about the birth of the church, in which the Spirit of God is breathed into Christ's body so that it becomes a living being, a recapitulation of Adam's creation in Genesis.

we be in a position to comprehend and accept the place of suffering in our lives, as we partake of the life of Christ.

OF THE MYSTICAL BODY OF CHRIST

We must now speak of that most wonderful and practical of doctrines: the mystical body of Christ. When I was a young man, I thought that ecclesiology (the part of theology which studies the church) was an expendable appendage to the body of theology; now, I believe that it is the very guts of theology.

Who are we as Christians? One ecclesiology says that the church is a collection of individual Christians with individual and private connections to Jesus Christ and that the church exists primarily to help individuals with their relationships with Jesus. Often, in such an ecclesiology, the church is seen as invisible and is not intended to intrude much into the larger culture or our daily lives.

In contrast, a true understanding of the mystical body of Jesus Christ is essential not only to a proper biblical theology but also to an understanding of human suffering and the seemingly impossible hope that it is redemptive, even in this life. The doctrine of the mystical body of Christ is the essence of what God has done and continues to do—to create and recreate man as a fit bride for him to marry and become one with. It is also the antidote to the disastrous individualism of the post-Reformation church and the answer to the neo-Gnostic "I'm spiritual but not religious" meme that is ubiquitous in the world, including the church, today.

The truth is: *How you see and treat the church is how you see and treat Jesus Christ.*

There are three bodies of Christ of which theologians speak. The first is the *natural body of Christ*, which was born of Mary, ministered in Israel for approximately thirty-three years, died, rose again, and has now ascended to the right hand of the Father. This is the natural body of Christ, which has taken on a new human nature and has lifted the New Humanity united to him into the heavenly places with him (Eph 2:6). It is the glorified natural body of Jesus that, after the resurrection, is human, isn't always recognized by his disciples, and can walk through walls.

The second body of Christ is the *mystical body of Christ*, which is the church. Why is it the *mystical* body of Christ? The word *mystical* seems doomed to conjure up men in wizard hats casting spells from entranced Lotus positions. But by "mystical" the church simply means "real but hidden."

The third body of Christ is the *Eucharistic body of Christ*, for the Scriptures teach that Jesus is truly present in the Eucharist and that those who are faithful members baptized into Christ are truly partakers of him in his Supper.

These three bodies of Christ are all united in ways that lie beyond the scope of my small book on suffering.

In contrast to the individualized and atomized Christ that we sometimes imagine, the Christ of the Scriptures gives not just spiritual gifts and talents and not just bits and pieces of a panoply of armor: He communicates his life to us. It's always tricky to say too much about such doctrines, but it's just as problematic to say too little.

It seems to work something like this: the divine and human nature are united in Jesus Christ, without the two losing their identities and becoming a *tertium quid*. In the same way, the church is united to Jesus Christ, without either of them losing its identity. The conclusion, then, is that God has united his divine nature to the *divinized* human nature of Jesus, a new human nature which he communicates to a redeemed humanity in some way.

This is what God as the husband of Israel, the Wedding Feast of the Lamb, and a man and a wife becoming one flesh are really all about. This is also what Saint Athanasius was getting at when he said: "God became man that man might become God."[3]

We sometimes have a mistaken sense of self-pity at the fact that things seemed so much more glamorous and miraculous in Bible times than today. But that pity and doubt melt away once we begin to comprehend the truth about the mystical body of Christ.

Think about it: only a small minority of the people who lived on earth at the time of Christ would ever have seen him. A small minority of those who lived in tiny Israel would have seen any of his miracles. Most of those who saw his miracles would have been privileged only to have seen one.

But if the church is truly the body of Christ, then think of the miracles, the preaching, and healing that Jesus does today! There are more than two billion Christians and hundreds of thousands of churches all across the world. Every time Christ comes to his people in the Eucharist, another miracle is performed, if only we had eyes to see. Every time a faithful preacher (even a poor one) preaches, Christ is preaching. Every time a Christian does good to someone else, Jesus is ministering to that person. This can only be true if, in some true sense, the church is Jesus Christ.

---

3. Athanasius, *Inc.* 54.

The church, therefore, is the prolongation or extension of the life of Jesus Christ through time and space. The scope of Christ's ministry is not merely the two billion Christians alive today but includes all of the things He has done or will do for men through men from the first chapters of the Scriptures until the time he returns!

Jesus is united to and never absent from his body, the church. The life and ministry that Jesus gave us for thirty-three years in Israel are now given to all Christians in all time and every place. The church is the new body of Christ that he assumed, by which he heals and saves the world today.

The church is also the physical, bodily presence of Jesus Christ on earth today. It's inconceivable that God would take the drastic and dramatic action of taking on human flesh for thirty-three years, only to seemingly abandon it for the next two thousand years. If the church is not the body of Christ, we're reduced to a hazy "spiritual" presence of Jesus in our lives and an invisible church and kingdom, of which no one can say "The kingdom of God is here!" or "Come and see!"

If the church is not the body of Christ, then we have no Jesus into whose hands and side we can put our hands to be convinced of his love.

Archbishop Fulton Sheen, with his usual elegance and eloquence, puts it this way:

> Were it not for the new Body, where would Christ have tongues with which to preach the Word of Life? Were it not for His Mystical Body, where would Christ find lips with which to speak forgiveness to penitent thieves? If it were not for this Body, where would He find hands to lay on little children, feet to receive the ointment of other Magdalenes, and a breast to receive the embrace of other Johns? . . . How else could He, as the incarnate God, console other widows than those of Nain, visit other friends than those of Bethany, attend other nuptials than those of Cana, call other apostles than those of the lake, convert other women than those in Samaria, and other men than the centurions of Calvary? How could He the God-man show meekness to other soldiers' executioners, patience to other timid disciples, love for other publicans, friendliness to other Judases, forgiveness to other malefactors, devotion to other Johns, affection to other Marys, wisdom to other doctors in the Law, except through another Body with whose Feet he could step from Jerusalem to the world, with whose lips He could speak to us to call ourselves modern?[4]

---

4. Sheen, *Mystical Body of Christ*, 51–52.

Archbishop Sheen adds:

> If we do not see him living to-day in his Mystical Body, then we would not have seen him living nineteen hundred years ago in His Physical Body. If we do not believe the Mystical Body to be divine, because it is also so human, then we would not have believed the Physical Body to be divine, because it was crucified. And if we miss the Lord Jesus it is not because he is too far away, but because he is too close.[5]

The meaning and importance of the related doctrines of the incarnation and the mystical body of Christ have been described in a way beyond compare by E. L. Mascall, who says:

> That in Jesus of Nazareth human nature is permanently and inseparably united to the Person of the Eternal Word, that by baptism men and women are re-created by incorporation into the human nature of Jesus and receive thereby a real communication of the benefits of His Passion, that sanctification is the progressive realization in the moral realm of the change that was made in the ontological realm by baptism, that incorporation into Christ is incorporation into the Church, since the Church is in its essence simply the human nature of Christ made appropriable by men, that all the thought, prayer and activity of Christians, in so far as it is brought within the sphere of redemption, is the act of Christ himself in and through the Church which is His body—these are the ideas that I have tried to expound; and the thread that unites them all is the doctrine of the permanence of the manhood of the glorified and ascended Christ.[6]

With these things in mind and heart, we must prepare ourselves for what lies ahead: that in baptism we are truly united to Jesus Christ, including not only his life and death but also his suffering. Let us go up to Jerusalem to die with Jesus!

> *The Church of God a kingdom is,*
> *where Christ in pow'r doth reign;*
> *where spirits yearn till, seen in bliss,*
> *their Lord shall come again.*
>
> *Glad companies of saints possess*
> *this Church below, above;*

---

5. Sheen, *Mystical Body of Christ*, 52.
6. Mascall, *Christ, the Christian, and the Church*, v.

The Second Cup, Part II

and God's perpetual calm doth bless
their paradise of love.

An altar stands within the shrine
whereon, once sacrificed,
is set, immaculate, divine,
the Lamb of God, the Christ.

There rich and poor, from countless lands,
praise God on mystic rood;
there nations reach forth holy hands
to take God's holy food.

There pure life-giving streams o'erflow
the sower's garden-ground;
and faith and hope fair blossoms show,
and fruits of love abound.

O King, O Christ, this endless grace
to all your people bring,
to see the vision of your face
in joy, O Christ, our King.
(Lionel Muirhead)

CHAPTER 2

We Are United to Christ Through Baptism

We are processing toward this thesis: "because Christ has become man and suffered to redeem man, suffering is a primary means of participating in God's nature and being united to him."

So far, we've accepted that the incarnation of Christ and the doctrine of the mystical body of Christ reveal that God has truly sought and truly created union with man. This union is effected through not only the incarnation but also the entire ministry of Jesus Christ, who is both God and man. Before we can be illuminated to see that we are united to Christ in his suffering, we must first recognize that a primary means of union with God is through holy baptism.[7]

We are especially united to Jesus Christ and his suffering through the sacrament of baptism. Saint Paul teaches:

> Or do you not know that as many of us as were baptized into Christ Jesus were baptized into His death? Therefore we were buried with Him through baptism into death, that just as Christ was raised from the dead by the glory of the Father, even so we also should walk in newness of life. For if we have been united together in the

---

7. Christians from some Christian traditions will disagree, but this was the clear consensus of the early church, the medieval church, and most of the magisterial Reformers. It is still the belief of a large majority of Christians, among whom are Roman Catholics, Orthodox Christians, Anglicans, Lutherans, and other Christians.

likeness of His death, certainly we also shall be in the likeness of His resurrection. (Rom 6:3–5)

We should not gloss too quickly over when Saint Paul teaches that baptism truly unites us to Jesus Christ. Paul's teaching, like the phrase "the body of Christ," is not merely figurative language. In baptism, God does something extraordinary to us.

In baptism you are born again, for baptism is the rebirth of which Jesus speaks. For this reason, baptism has also been called "regeneration," although that term is now much cloudier than it used to be. The early church even called baptism the "illumination" and "enlightenment." In baptism, the traditional *Book of Common Prayer* catechism tells us, you were made "a member of Christ, the child of God, and an inheritor of the kingdom of heaven."

Our chief focus here is on being made a member of the body of Christ. Saint Paul employs this language commonly, for example, when speaking of the proper use of spiritual gifts in Romans 12, 1 Corinthians 6 and 12, and Ephesians 5. For this reason, because we are members of that one body, Paul often says that we are *in* Christ, as members are in a body.

In fact, in baptism, we are given our eternal identity: baptism makes us Christians and identifies us to the world, both visible and invisible, as Christians, or "little Christs." Everyone today is looking for an identity: we've all heard of people having identity crises. You can see it in the way people change their hair or cars or even their lifestyles, searching for their "true" identity.

For the Christian, the new identity that God gives us in baptism is that of Jesus Christ.

By your baptism, you were made a new creature—a creature fit again to relate to God because you are in union with Jesus Christ, the Son. You are now someone able, like God, to live in love. God has adopted you into his blessed family, and you have the privilege of calling God "Our Father" because of your union with the Son of God.

Being united to Jesus Christ in baptism means, therefore, that we are *partakers* of Christ. He shares or communicates with us his divinized human nature so that, in a mysterious way, he becomes one with us: He in us and we in him.[8]

---

8. Baptism doesn't work in a vacuum. The life of Christ that is given by God in baptism is sustained and nurtured only by a life of faithfulness in a living relationship with God and his church.

Great is the mystery of the incarnation!

Great is the mystery of baptism!

For the life of the Holy Trinity—the Father, the Son, and the Holy Spirit—is forever united to the human nature of Christ by his incarnation. Jesus has shared his divinized human nature with his body and bride, the church, so that she (and her members) and he are one.

In baptism, Christ incorporates Christians into his nature and life, which is united to the Godhead. The union baptized Christians have with Christ and, therefore, with God, is very real!

Baptism, first Christ's and then ours, is closely related to the death and resurrection of Jesus Christ. When Jesus descended into the waters of his baptism, he immersed himself in the chaos of death, for water became in the Bible a picture of judgment (for example, the deluge and the crossing of the Red Sea). In the beginning, however, the creative Spirit was hovering over the waters of creation, and so Jesus's baptism is also an act of the New Creation and the New Man.

At his baptism, Jesus entered into union with sinful men and the suffering of which they all partake. For this reason, Jesus equates his own suffering, which culminates in his crucifixion, with his baptism, saying: "But I have a baptism to be baptized with, and how distressed I am till it is accomplished!" (Luke 12:50).

All of this means that contained in Jesus's baptism is the promise of first his death and then his resurrection.

Our baptism pictures the same thing: the death and resurrection of Christ, which is the death and resurrection of man, which is the death and resurrection of each baptized Christian. The Eucharist, likewise, is a participation in both the death and resurrection of Christ, of which we were first made partakers in our baptisms.

For a Christian to be baptized, therefore, means the death and resurrection of that member of the body of Christ. But this death cannot and will not take place without suffering. For Jesus to conquer all of man's enemies—Satan, sin, suffering, and death—he must wrestle with and conquer them. His victory over them comes only at the price of his own suffering, including the ultimate suffering of death.

The entire chapter of Mark 10 instructs us in how the life of Christ communicated to us is a life of suffering. In Mark 10, Jesus is teaching his disciples about the nature of his kingdom, that it is composed of those such as little children; that those who are like the rich young ruler will not enter the kingdom; and that he is about to go up to Jerusalem where he will be betrayed and put to death.

The response of the disciples provokes Jesus's teaching on baptismal suffering. James and John, in spite of Jesus's teaching about childlikeness, humility, and poverty, ask for positions of glory and power in Christ's kingdom. Jesus asks them: "Are you able to drink the cup that I drink, and be baptized with the baptism that I am baptized with?" (v. 38). He follows this up by revealing that: "You will indeed drink the cup that I drink, and with the baptism I am baptized with you will be baptized" (v. 39). Thus, we see that life in Christ's kingdom (which is nothing less than life in Christ) will mean suffering.

James and John were not wrong to seek the kingdom and the glory and the power when they asked Jesus if they could sit on his right and left hand. After all, when they asked this in Mark 9, they had just seen Jesus transfigured and reasoned that this was their eternal destiny in Christ. But James and John, like Peter before them (after his great confession), couldn't see what Jesus intended: that it was only through suffering that they, in Christ, would be raised to glory.

They would, indeed, be baptized with Christ's baptism and drink with him his cup, but they could not see, before the gift of the Holy Spirit, that the glory of Christ's kingdom comes by both baptismal suffering and eucharistic suffering. United to Christ in baptism, the disciples of Jesus will suffer and die. United to Christ in the Eucharist, Jesus's disciples' will suffer and die. Only through these things will the kingdom, with its attendant glory and power, come.

Baptism, therefore, is the initial and essential means by which we are united to the life of Jesus Christ. Incorporated into Christ and his body through baptism, we are united with Christ, who has taken all human suffering and transformed its evil into a means of union with himself, and, therefore, into a means of glory and joy.

As we process toward the heart of the mystery of human suffering transformed by Christ, we experience yet another shock of recognition: that God has such high regard for the value of man that he has recruited and commissioned man to partake of his holy work of redemption.

God has chosen not to save man without using men to do so.

God is using a new humanity, united to the New Man, Christ, as the instrument of his salvation. Apparently, God thinks man is worthy of redemption and, even more, that man's place in God's creation is so high that he won't save us without us being a part of his work of salvation. How else could it be, if God has intended to take man as his bride in the New Heavens and New Earth?

To be caught up in God's holy work of redemption, however, necessarily means being caught up in the sufferings of the incarnate Christ.

> *We yield thee hearty thanks, most merciful Father, that it hath pleased thee to regenerate us with thy Holy Spirit, to receive us for thine own Children, and to incorporate us into thy holy Church. And humbly we beseech thee to grant, that we, being dead unto sin, may live unto righteousness, and being buried with Christ in his death, may also be partakers of his resurrection; so that finally, with the residue of thy holy Church, we may be inheritors of thine everlasting kingdom; through Christ our Lord. Amen.*
> (Adapted from the 1928 *Book of Common Prayer*)

CHAPTER 3

Baptized Christians are United to All of Christ

When we are united to Christ in baptism, therefore, we are united to *all* of Christ: first, the life of suffering for Christ, then the crucifixion, and only then the resurrection and ascension. United to Christ, we recapitulate his life. For this reason, the consistent biblical pattern of our lives is that *suffering, afflictions, and trials lead to glory and joy for the Christian,* which is the exuberant thesis of this book.

The most significant meaning for Christian suffering is this: *united to Christ by baptism, we become real partakers of the divinized human nature of Jesus Christ. Since Jesus suffered for us, we suffer with, in, through, and for him, for we are genuinely "in" Christ.*

Man is now born (though not originally so) to suffer. Either he will suffer, on the one hand, for the evil that entered the world through the first Adam, or he will suffer for the good that entered the world through the Second Adam.

You and I suffer as men because we are united to the first Adam, who suffers privation of good as a consequence of being excommunicated from the life of God. When we suffer apart from Christ, we are partaking of the fallenness of creation, the deprivation of all the good that was once our birthright. This is the terrible consequence of man walking away from the Good that is God himself. We suffer in this way as a consequence of sin, by which we turn good into evil.

Baptized Christians are United to All of Christ

But there is another kind of suffering by which evil is turned into good. This is the suffering of the Second Adam. While the first kind of suffering was not chosen by man, the Second Adam chooses the second kind of suffering to undo the evil of the first.

You and I suffer, if we have been baptized into Christ, because we suffer in our bodies as the mystical body of Christ which suffers with the natural body of Christ.

Your body is not your own, Saint Paul teaches: it was bought by and belongs to God (1 Cor 6:19–20). The body of the Christian belongs to Christ, not only in the sense that he owns it by virtue of having redeemed or bought it, but also because the body of each Christian is a member of the one body of Jesus Christ. The greatest delusion of all is that to think that you are an individual Christian, independent from other Christians. The truth is that your suffering is the sacrament of the suffering of the body of Christ, not only his natural body on the cross and in his passion but also the suffering of his mystical body, the church.

The great transmutation of evil into good can only be accomplished by experiencing the loss of all things for Christ. And this turns out to be a painful process. We believe that we are healed by *his* wounds (Isa 53:5; 1 Pet 2:24). But if we are united to Christ and partake of all of Christ, then we, too, will suffer. And if we are united to Christ and his work, then our suffering, too, proves to be redemptive. We might even be so bold as to say that "By *our* wounds we are healed," as long as we understand that our suffering has no redemptive value apart from its partaking of Christ and his suffering.

It turns out that when Christ became man, he was not only doing something *for* us but was also doing something *to* us. What he is doing is giving birth to the New Man, the New Creation.

Just as the first, natural birth is painful, so is the second, supernatural, birth painful. *All of the suffering of Christians is the birth pangs of Christ preparing a body for himself and is the birth of the New Man.*

As Saint Paul teaches us: "For we know that the whole creation groans and labors with birth pangs together until now. Not only that, but we also who have the firstfruits of the Spirit, even we ourselves groan within ourselves, eagerly waiting for the adoption, the redemption of our body" (Rom 8:22–23).

But in the life to come, and even in this life to some degree, we rejoice that a New Man has been born in us, Christ the Risen One. As Jesus assures us:

> I say to you that you will weep and lament, but the world will rejoice; and you will be sorrowful, but your sorrow will be turned into joy. A woman, when she is in labor, has sorrow because her hour has come; but as soon as she has given birth to the child, she no longer remembers the anguish, for joy that a human being has been born into the world (John 16:20–21).

This new birth, this deliverance into the kingdom of light, will be a painful process, for Jesus Christ is himself the kingdom. Once this truth is grasped, it's easy to see why Christians suffer: we can only enter into the kingdom through tribulation, since this is the way Christ himself entered. Everything we said earlier about how Christ's glory was manifested precisely in his suffering applies as well to us, who are in Christ.

That Christians must enter the kingdom through tribulation and suffering is exemplified not only in the life of Jesus but also that of Saint Paul. Paul, when still called Saul, caused much suffering in Christ and his disciples, and he would himself suffer much for Christ. When Jesus called Saul, he told Ananias, concerning Saul: "I will show him how many things he must suffer for My name's sake" (Acts 9:16).

United to Jesus, Paul also experienced a resurrection of his own, for example, in Acts 14 where we read: "Then Jews from Antioch and Iconium came there; and having persuaded the multitudes, they stoned Paul and dragged him out of the city, supposing him to be dead. However, when the disciples gathered around him, he rose up and went into the city" (Acts 14:19–20).

Notice how Paul is executed by the Jews like Jesus and, like Jesus, is dragged out of the city. As with Jesus, the resurrected Paul appears in the midst of the disciples.

Why does Paul suffer so much?[9] It's because Paul was united to Jesus, which meant a share of his suffering. For this reason, Paul's greatest desire was "that I may know Him and the power of His resurrection, and the fellowship of His sufferings, being conformed to His death, if, by any means, I may attain to the resurrection from the dead" (Phil 3:10–11).

The New Birth is also a painful process because all Christian suffering is purgatorial, in that all suffering in this life is part of the redemptive process of purging us of our sins and turning evil into good.[10] To come into the presence of the Lord who is a consuming fire is painful because it

---

9. See, for example, 2 Cor 11:23–29.
10. No comment on the afterlife is necessarily implied.

purges away part of us, and any surgery, cauterization, or transplantation is a painful process. It's painful as well because our loving Father is not punishing us but disciplining, correcting, and forging us. It is painful for someone already formed to be reformed into someone new.

Unfortunately, a most common assumption Christians have about suffering is that it is either God punishing them or something that is to be born stoically. Too infrequently is suffering seen by the Christian for what it truly is: a means of union with Jesus! This suffering of ours, which we may also call "bearing the cross," is actually a sign that we are united to Jesus, partake of him, and, indeed, belong to him.

For in baptism, we have been united to Christ, and this means *all* of Christ: His life, his death, his resurrection, his ascension, his reign, and—yes—his *suffering*.

We find in Calvin's *Institutes* the very thing we have been saying, as well as some of the things we shall soon say:

> Why should we exempt ourselves, therefore, from the condition to which Christ our Head had to submit, especially since he submitted to it for our sake to show us an example of patience in himself? Therefore, the apostle teaches that God has destined all his children to the end that they be conformed to Christ [Rom 8:29]. Hence also in harsh and difficult conditions, regarded as adverse and evil, a great comfort comes to us: we share Christ's sufferings in order that as he has passed from a labyrinth of all evils into heavenly glory, we may in like manner be led through various tribulations to the same glory [Acts 14:22].
>
> So Paul himself elsewhere states: when we come to know the sharing of his sufferings, we at the same time grasp the power of his resurrection; and when we become like him in his death, we are thus made ready to share his glorious resurrection [Phil 3:10–11]. How much can it do to soften all the bitterness of the cross, that the more we are afflicted with adversities, the more surely our fellowship with Christ is confirmed! By communion with him the very sufferings themselves not only become blessed to us but also help much in promoting our salvation (*Institutes*, Book 3, Chapter 8, Section 1).

The church, therefore, as the body of Christ, continues to live out the grace-filled, Spirit-filled life of Jesus Christ, or, rather, he continues to live in and through us. The mysteries of God in us—the incarnation, the church, the sacraments, and suffering and joy—are inseparable. Because we are the body of Christ, Jesus continues to suffer with us and transform our suffering from mere human suffering into the goodness of God that unites us to him. And yet at the same time, Jesus is forever risen from the dead, which means, of course, that we are also risen with him.

So, then, as long as this world continues, we see these things at work in us simultaneously: the suffering and death of Jesus Christ, as well as his resurrection, glory, and joy.

> *Lord Jesus Christ, who willingly gave up all things for me and for the salvation of the world, give me a fervent desire to seek You above everything else in my life. Help me to be willing to give up the things that lead me away from You and the things that are not good for my soul that I might know the fellowship of Your sufferings and the power and joy of Your resurrection. Amen.* (Charles Erlandson)

CHAPTER 4

The Eucharistic Body, Holy Communion, and Suffering

What God has Joined Together, Let Not Man Separate

BAPTISM LEADS TO EUCHARIST

While in baptism we are incorporated into the body of Jesus Christ, in the Eucharist,[11] the life of this body is sustained and fed by him who is the Bread of Life and life everlasting. Just as the cross and resurrection can never be separated, baptism and the Eucharist cannot be separated, for together they communicate to us the life of Jesus Christ. Both baptism and Eucharist proclaim, represent, and partake of both the crucifixion and resurrection of Jesus Christ.

Not only do baptism and the Eucharist belong together, but also the three bodies of Jesus Christ of which we have spoken earlier: the natural body of Christ, the mystical body of Christ, and the Eucharistic body of Christ. That natural, glorified body of Jesus Christ (and not just his body but his entire human nature) is one with his mystical body the church,

---

11. Throughout this book I'll be using the name "Eucharist," which was the preferred name given to the holy meal by the early church. Equivalent terms are the Holy Communion, the Lord's Supper, and the Mass, all of which express other important aspects of this special covenantal meal of Jesus with his disciples.

and both of these are one with the Eucharistic body of Christ, by which he makes himself present in his supper and communicates himself to us.

We have no need to enter into disputes about the manner by which Christ truly gives himself to his body in the Eucharist: the early church was generally content to believe that it was so.

The crucifixion and resurrection, and the suffering and joy which are bound together by God in this life, are all part of the significance of the Eucharist. For in partaking of the Eucharist, we are, as Saint Paul teaches, proclaiming Christ's death until he returns. But that death never stands alone, not even at the moment of Christ's expiration. Christ's death and resurrection only have meaning in relation to each other.

At the same time we proclaim Christ's death in the Lord's Supper, we also celebrate his resurrection on the Lord's Day. Death, in this sense, is swallowed up by life. At the cross, God swallowed our suffering, consumed it, and transformed it into life: as we have said, God takes the evil and suffering of this world and transmutes them into Good. In the Eucharist, likewise, God swallows our suffering, consumes it, and transforms it into himself, which he then gives back to us.

The resurrection is hidden in the remembrance of the cross and its sacrifice, and the promise of the resurrection is implicit in and revealed by the cross. The two always go together, especially on the Lord's Day. The day Christ rose from the dead, and the day which is now the sign of Christ's resurrected presence with us, is also the day we celebrate his suffering sacrifice.

THE BREAD AND THE WINE

As the cross and the resurrection, and suffering and joy, always go together, so do the bread and the wine of the Eucharist. The bread and the wine *together* represent and communicate the body and blood of Christ, not one separated from the other. Throughout the Scriptures, both bread and wine have numerous theological associations that are brought together in the Eucharist. Because Jesus focuses on the cup, both when discussing the kingdom with James and John (Matt 20) and in the agony in the garden (Matt 26), our primary focus in this book is on the cup. Nevertheless, in this chapter, we will discuss the symbolism of both the bread and the wine.

Every Christian knows that the bread and wine of the Eucharist represent the body and blood of Jesus Christ, even when we differ in our interpretations about how and to what degree Christ is present in his supper.

But in the bread and wine, which is the body and blood of Jesus Christ, the gospel of suffering is also taught.

Bread and wine are fit representatives of Christ's body and blood. This is so because of the solid, fleshly nature of both bread and body and the red, liquid nature of both wine and blood. But there are more substantial truths here for us to digest as well. Both bread and wine represent the unity in multiplicity that is the nature of the triune God. One loaf of bread is made from the grains of wheat of many wheat plants. One chalice of wine is made from the grapes of many grapevines.

The church has recognized this nature of bread and wine from the beginning, as evidenced from this passage from the Didache (c. AD 70–100): "As this broken bread was scattered over the hills and then, when gathered, became one mass, so may Thy Church be gathered from the ends of the earth into Thy Kingdom."[12]

Both bread and wine, like Christ's body and blood, give us life. This is a mundane miracle, but two things keep us from seeing daily miracles: scientism (the belief that science provides ultimate meaning) and ubiquity. We're trained by our culture and schools to believe that the scientific interpretation of the meaning of things is the only valid one. Because of this, the sun becomes a "yellow dwarf star of average size, mass, age, and luminosity," instead of what it more truly is: the brilliant, luminescent light in the sky which reminds us of and partakes of the glory of the Son of God.

We also miss out on daily miracles precisely because they are daily. It's incorrect to think of miracles as merely something God does that breaks the laws of nature (as if nature is a god whom God must obey), or God working in uncustomary ways. God's customary way of working *is* a miracle, for miracles are visible signs of the presence of God.

What's more, food could have been the pinkish-grey stew of Orwell's *1984* or the food cubes of *Star Trek*. We eat not mechanically or joylessly but with gusto and meaning. Why? Isn't eating just a necessary biological function?

Food is not just food: it is a lesser sacrament. Clearly, it's a matter of life and death, for it brought death to Adam and Eve and their gluttonous progeny but brings life to those who eat the flesh and blood of Jesus Christ.

Food is for fun: it is delightful, enjoyable, scrumptious, and delectable. Where good food and drink abound, the music of singing and laughter is not far behind. Food is enticing. It is so good that we are tempted, like Eve,

---

12. Did. 9.

to make an idol out of it, or to think in this modern world that it just gets here magically.

Food is for fulfillment: after a good meal, we are sated and satisfied, full and fulfilled, and don't need or want anything more.

Food is for fellowship: men are meant to eat in communion with one another. This is why, in the ancient world, men would not eat with those with whom they were at war. For this reason, also, Jews and gentiles would not share table fellowship. But all men are now able to eat together at Christ's table because in Christ there is no Greek or Jew, male or female, slave or free. This human table fellowship flows from the more substantial fellowship we now share with God in his house at his meal.

The food of the bread and wine, which is both human and divine, is the perfect creature to act as the sacrament of God's life-giving gift of his Son.

THE SACRIFICE OF BREAD AND WINE

By the marvelous way that both the bread and the wine give themselves to us through a process of life and death, they picture the way Christ gives Himself to us. This is wondrously expressed for us by Archbishop Fulton Sheen when he writes:

> No two substances in nature have to suffer more to become what they are than bread and wine. Wheat has to pass through the rigors of winter, be ground beneath the Calvary of a mill, and then subjected to purging fire before it can become bread. Grapes in their turn must be subjected to the Gethsemane of a wine press and have their life crushed from them to become wine. Thus, do they symbolize the Passion and Sufferings of Christ, and the condition of Salvation, for Our Lord said unless we die to ourselves we cannot live in Him[13]

Nature teaches us the principle of death and resurrection. Every night and day, we rehearse our own resurrection, for every night we ritually die as we fall asleep, and every morning we are raised from the dead by God.

Nature itself also teaches the principle of sacrifice, that one gives of oneself for the life of another. Surely this is the meaning of Jesus's teaching when he says: "Most assuredly, I say to you, unless a grain of wheat falls into the ground and dies, it remains alone; but if it dies, it produces much grain. He who loves his life will lose it, and he who hates his life in this world will

---

13. Sheen, *Life of Christ*, 278.

keep it for eternal life" (John 12:24–25). As Sheen puts it: "Nature, He said, was stamped with a Cross: death is the condition of new life."[14]

All created things are constantly offering themselves up for the lives of other things, in God's good creation. Fulton Sheen, once again, expresses it this way:

> Unless the plants sacrifice themselves to being plucked up from the roots, they cannot nourish or commune with man. The sacrifice of what is lowest must precede communion with what is higher. First His death was mystically represented; then communion followed. The lower is transformed into the higher; chemicals into plants; plants into animals; chemicals, plants, and animals into man; and man into Christ by communion.[15]

Just as bread and wine give themselves up so that they may become our human bodies, in a similar manner, Christians give themselves up to God so that they may become, in his hands, the body of Jesus Christ. Some Christians worry about calling the Eucharist a sacrifice: they're fearful that such an admission will lead one straight into a notion of a re-sacrificed Christ. But this need not be the case, for surely sacrifice is present all throughout the Eucharist.

Saint Paul tells us that whenever we partake of the Eucharist, we are proclaiming Christ's death (which is to say, his *sacrifice*) until his coming again (1 Cor 11:26). Paul also tells us that those who serve at the altar are partakers of the sacrifice (1 Cor 9:13). How can there be any doubt that Jesus continues to give himself in love to his bride? This giving of self to another is what we call love: it is also what we call sacrifice. Every time Jesus celebrates his feast with us, he humiliates himself, offers himself to us, and descends to us once again.

But there is another sacrifice present at the altar, and that sacrifice is us. We look around, ask with Isaac, "Where is the sacrifice?" and then come to the joyful but costly realization that we are also the sacrifice! By prayer and thanksgiving, by our tithes and offerings, and by the giving of our bodies and souls to the Lord, we become a living sacrifice that is united to Christ's.

What are these conjoined oblations but the love of God, the giving up of self, which God shares with us through suffering?

---

14. Sheen, *Life of Christ*, 266.
15. Sheen, *Life of Christ*, 280.

In the end, we experience a great transformation in the Eucharist. What actually happens is that when our sacrifice or oblation is joined with Christ's through the partaking of Christ's sacrifice in the Eucharist, *we become Christ*. Perhaps, it's not so much that the bread and wine become the body and blood of Christ: it's that *our* body and blood become the body and blood of Christ as he makes us one flesh with himself. Christ is not just in the bread and wine: *He's in us!* God in us, Immanuel!

In the Eucharist, when we consume the Lord who has given himself to us as heavenly food, we become the body of Jesus Christ. Through the bread of the broken grain and the wine of the crushed grapes, we become one in the body of Christ. This is the true and greater transubstantiation. Truly, *you are what you eat*!

This great transformation should not be so surprising. When bread and wine are taken into us, they are changed into the bodies and blood of men. When Jesus takes bread and wine, he changes them into himself. The great transformation of food into men and God into food is the truest reason we eat and enjoy food.

But when I partake of the Eucharist, more astonishing things happen. When I offer up myself to Christ, as he has first offered himself to me, my eyes brighten as if I had satisfied myself with divine honey. I experience shock and awe when I realize that *I* am crushed with grape and grain. *I*, with Christ, am the sacrifice.

It is not just I who consume Christ, and I who become a part of him: He also consumes me! He takes me into himself, digests, or breaks me down, and then makes me a part of his body. But, like the grape and grain, I can only become a part of his body if I am first willing to die to be with him and in him. And this is why becoming one with Jesus will necessarily involve suffering.

But when the Father sees our meager sacrifice of self, he has mercy on our widow's mite because, in it, he sees the inexhaustible riches of Christ's payment for us. When God the Father sees us, he sees his Son and pours out on us the love which he has had for the Son before the creation of the world.

THE JUDGMENT OF BREAD AND WINE

Judgment is a two-edged sword. The sufferings of those in Christ and those not in Christ look the same from the outside but have radically different meanings inside. The waters of baptism look just like earthly water to the unbeliever but are for Christians the waters of life. The bread and wine of the Eucharist look like earthly food and drink to the unbeliever but are for Christians the bread of life and the living water.

So it is with our suffering. There is no promise in the Bible that Christians will not suffer or that they will escape tribulation. Quite the opposite! Everywhere the assumption is that Christians, in union with and in imitation of their Lord, *will* suffer. Just as the rain falls on the just and unjust alike, so do the evils of this world. But the meaning of the suffering and evil experienced by the Christian, in union with Christ, is radically unlike that of unbelievers.

Some theologians have expressed the belief that both believers and unbelievers will experience the same presence of the Lord in the afterlife. But the difference is this: while God's presence for Christians will be complete joy and blessing, for unbelievers, Satan, and the demons, the continued presence of God will be loathsome.

Judgment is a two-edged sword. The pain of suffering may feel the same to believer and unbeliever alike, but the significances and consequences are quite different. Suffering, for those who are not united to Christ, continues to be the punishment of God upon wicked evildoers who remain the enemies of God. But for those in Christ, who are members of the body of Christ, suffering is transformed into the loving discipline and correction of the Father.

This is what the writer of the letter to the Hebrews means when he writes:

> If you endure chastening, God deals with you as with sons; for what son is there whom a father does not chasten? But if you are without chastening, of which all have become partakers, then you are illegitimate and not sons. Furthermore, we have had human fathers who corrected us, and we paid them respect. Shall we not much more readily be in subjection to the Father of spirits and live? For they indeed for a few days chastened us as seemed best to them, but He for our profit, that we may be partakers of His holiness. Now no chastening seems to be joyful for the present, but painful; nevertheless, afterward it yields the peaceable fruit of righteousness to those who have been trained by it. (Heb 12:7–11)

Suffering, for the Christian, means God is treating us as his beloved children. He who did not spare the rod to his own Son will not spare it on us, who are the children of God by virtue of our life in Christ. Suffering, for the Christian, means that God the Father is treating us as he did his Son. But the chastisement of the Son was something God voluntarily took upon himself: it is something God does to himself for us. Like the grapes and the wheat, Christ willingly gave up his life that we might have life.

Suffering, therefore, is God's judgment and proclamation that baptized Christians are united to the Son, who is also the Suffering Servant.

Blood means death. For when the blood, which is the life, is drained from the sacrificial animal, the animal can live no longer. There's a reason most of us don't like to see blood seeping, oozing, pouring, or gushing from our bodies: we know that its departure might well mean our own. To separate the blood from the body means death.

But blood means life even more than it means death. For as the Bible teaches, "the life is in the blood" (Lev 19:11), and it's actually the absence of blood that causes death. A blood sacrifice means that someone gives his life for the good of another. It is this self-giving ("love") that enables blood to have its cleansing power. For the blood represents the life of something or someone given for the good of another. This is what gives blood its sanctifying, purifying, and atoning power, as discussed, for example, in Hebrews 9.

The new covenant, like the old, was sealed with blood because blood is a sign of life. Those who partake of the blood by staining their hands in it are partakers not only of the life of the one whose blood was given but also of all who also touch the common blood.

And so the wine represents for us both the death and the life of Jesus Christ, whose life was given for the life of the world. While we look at blood, separated from the body, and only see death, God sees the blood in the body of his beloved Son and sees only life.

Not only wine but also bread is a sign and instrument of life. Food, by its very nature, is a sacrament of God, being a means by which God blesses us and gives us life. In doing so, God gives himself to all men in love. Food is, perhaps, the best mnemonic device to remind us of God and his goodness, which is why saying grace before meals, as paltry a thing to do as it may seem, is profoundly sacramental and blessed.

When God wanted to reveal himself to the Israelites in the wilderness, he chose a form of bread: manna. But Jesus is the Bread of Life which brings eternal life.

Bread represents life not only in its material dimension but also in its spiritual sense. When we ask God every day for our daily bread in the

Lord's Prayer, we are most truly asking for Jesus himself, who is the Bread of Life and our Daily Bread. This Daily Bread, which is Christ, is also the source of every other kind of bread or need with which God fills us.

But to ask for our daily bread, which means to ask for Jesus, is to ask for more than we imagine. For we find that if we pray this prayer with faith, God will give us Christ. But he will give us *all* of Christ, including his suffering and self-giving. How can it be otherwise, for what was the daily bread of Jesus? Jesus tells us that: "My food is to do the will of Him who sent Me, and to finish His work" (John 4:34). But what was the will of the Father for the Son? It was to suffer and give himself in all of the ways we mentioned earlier[16] when concluding that the entirety of Jesus's life was a self-giving sacrifice that caused him to suffer. The will of the loving Father, even at the point of Christ's anguished plea in the second garden, was for him to suffer and die for the life of the world.

And so when we ask for our daily bread, the Father will, indeed, give us Jesus. But he will give us the suffering Jesus whose bread is to do the will of the Father—and the will of the Father is that we give ourselves to him and to others in love.

And this, of necessity, involves suffering.

We will find this suffering, this obedience, our daily bread in which Christ dwells, in all of our "trivial rounds and common tasks." We will constantly encounter Jesus and be blessed by him if we can see him and his call for sacrifice in the thousand small ways we must give up ourselves and not only the occasional works of "supererogation."

Each day God serves us this morsel of truth: *"the daily grind makes the daily bread."*

THE EVER-PRESENT EUCHARIST

"And as they were eating, Jesus took the bread, blessed, and broke it, and gave it to them and said, 'Take, eat; this is My body'" (Matt 26:26).

In a moment of time that encompasses all time, as Christ breaks the bread, he *has broken* it, he *breaks* it, and he *will break* it: time takes the form of our ancient and venerable history; it smacks us in the face as a present force; and it whispers to us of what will always be.

As we see Jesus take the bread, we see Jesus's birth and incarnation. God takes hold of his creation and becomes a part of it so that he might

---

16. See the Second Cup, Part I, chapter 5.

redeem it. As we see the priest take hold of the bread, we see Jesus take hold of the bread. The incarnation is present here at the Eucharist, and God once again pronounces over his creation, "It is good, it is *very* good!"

As we hear Jesus bless the bread, we sense his holy and perfect life. The birth of Christ is forever connected to the life of Christ: God blesses what he took hold of for us, whether human life, or the bread of the earth, or the Bread of Life that unites them both. The Son didn't become man only to die but also to live, and by that holy life that he took and lived out, we are made holy as well.

As we see the bread be broken and hear the snap or the quiet bend of its moment of brokenness, we hear and see the coming crucifixion. Here, as the bread is broken, the body of the Bread of Life is also broken—broken two thousand years and broken forever as the one, sufficient, and perfect sacrifice for the life of the world. Here is Christ's sacrifice: once broken and always broken; once offered and always offered.

The hour of Christ, which he shares with us, is not only his time on the cross but also the Eucharist.

As we feel the bread when our turn to partake arrives, we feel the resurrection, ascension, and Pentecost of Christ. Here is the life of Christ, who though he was dead now lives again. Here is the resurrection, promising that after the life of Christ has been offered and taken, He will take it up again. Here is the ascension, promising that the human life which Christ first took hold of has now been glorified and has entered heaven, the divine and human dwelling together forever in unity. Here is the Pentecost of Christ, the life of Christ given for the body of Christ, for as Christ is broken in the Eucharist and on the cross and ascends into heaven, he is miraculously multiplied as the members of Christ are knit together into the one body.

In the Eucharist, we *remember* with *faith* what God has done through the death and life of the Son.

In the Eucharist, we *partake*, with *love*, of the Son, who is truly present with us at the moment of eating and drinking.

In the Eucharist, we *imagine* with *hope* the promised blessings of the life to come which is both the Marriage Supper of the Lamb and the Beatific Vision, for, as with the disciples on the road to Emmaus, in eating Jesus with Jesus, our eyes and every other sense are opened. The Eucharist unites us to all of Christ: His sacrifice, his resurrection, and his life.

The Eucharistic Body, Holy Communion, and Suffering

The sobering fact remains that while we partake of the life to come in the Eucharist, God is still in the process of redeeming the cosmos. This means that the Eucharist will remain not only a sign of and participation in Christ's complete victory and bliss in the life to come but also a sign of and participation in the means by which Christ gains this victory: suffering, struggle, self-surrender, sacrifice, and death.

When my mother was a young girl, she joined the Loyal Temperance Union, the children's arm of the WCTU (Women's Christian Temperance Union), and took an oath never to drink alcohol. She has kept this vow admirably well. The one exception she has made is when she comes to my Reformed Episcopal Church and partakes of the cup of wine. Being used to grape juice, the first time she took the cup of wine, she exclaimed: "It burned all the way down!"

And so when we drink the cup of purgation, the cup of Christ's suffering, the cup which transmutes evil into good and fallen men into the likeness of Christ, it burns all the way down.

This, by the way, is how you know something good is happening.

> *All glory be to thee, Almighty God, our heavenly Father, for that thou, of thy tender mercy, didst give thine only Son Jesus Christ to suffer death upon the Cross for our redemption; who made there (by his one oblation of himself once offered) a full, perfect, and sufficient sacrifice, oblation, and satisfaction, for the sins of the whole world; and did institute, and in his holy Gospel command us to continue, a perpetual memory of that his precious death and sacrifice, until his coming again.*
>
> *We most heartily thank thee, for that thou dost vouchsafe to feed us who have duly received these holy mysteries, with the spiritual food of the most precious Body and Blood of thy Son our Saviour Jesus Christ; and dost assure us thereby of thy favour and goodness towards us; and that we are very members incorporate in the mystical body of thy Son, which is the blessed company of all faithful people; and are also heirs through hope of thy everlasting kingdom, by the merits of his most precious death and passion. And we humbly beseech thee, O heavenly Father, so to assist us with thy grace, that we may continue in that holy fellowship, and do all such good works as thou hast prepared for us to walk in; through Jesus Christ our Lord, to whom, with thee and the Holy Ghost, be all honour and glory, world without end. Amen.* (Prayer of Consecration, traditional *Book of Common Prayer*)

CHAPTER 5

Suffering Is a Sacrament of Christ's Presence

The sacraments of baptism and Holy Communion, which we explored in chapters 3 and 4, are sacraments of the blessed presence of Jesus Christ in the lives of believers, by which we are truly united to him. By the sacraments we are united to the whole Christ, including not only his life but also his death and suffering. We may, therefore, conclude that suffering is a sacrament of Christ and of God's presence, goodness, and kingdom, for it is a visible means of partaking of Christ.

Christ suffered for us. But because we are spiritually and mystically united to him as the body of Christ, we will suffer. The suffering of the church is a sign that we belong to Jesus Christ. When the church suffers for Jesus Christ, it must be because the Lord is near, very near—so near that what is true for him is true for us.

The suffering of the church is a sacrament, in the lesser sense of that word, because it is not just a reminder that Jesus suffered for us but also a true *participation* in Christ and his sufferings. It is a participation in Christ's loving suffering for us, and how could we truly know the love of God and his suffering for us unless we, too, suffered?

His cross is our cross, and our crosses are his. We are, therefore, bound together by suffering. For this reason, Saint Paul prays "that I may know Him and the power of His resurrection, and the fellowship of His

Suffering Is a Sacrament of Christ's Presence

sufferings, being conformed to His death, if, by any means, I may attain to the resurrection from the dead" (Phil 3:10).

Our suffering is Christ's suffering, and his suffering is ours.

This means that when we suffer, as members of his suffering body, we each carry with us a splinter of the one true cross. Unlike the medieval forgeries of the splinters of the cross, each Christian who suffers is carrying a holy relic, a splinter of the suffering of Christ on the cross.

God's blessed and mighty redemption for us is, therefore, something he not only does *for* us but also *through* us, for we are the body of Christ, and God has made us partakers of his nature and redemption.

If God's redemption were simply something he did *to* us, we'd be rocks.

If his redemption were something he did *for* us, we'd be children.

If God's redemption were something he did *with* us, we'd be men.

But since God's redemption is something he does *through* us, we are members of Christ's body.

Because of this, the church also suffers *as Christ*, united to him as his body.

If Christ is with us in our suffering this way, transforming it into his glory, then Christ is in all things for the Christian!

Suffering is sacramental: it is a means by which we are united to Jesus.

> *Father, thank You for entrusting Your glory to such weak and earthen vessels as myself. Help me to remember that while suffering is visible and momentary, joy and glory are eternal, even when not visible. I ask, Jesus, that You would take my pain and suffering today and carry it with me, and that You might help me to see You and share in Your resurrection and life today.* (Charles Erlandson)

CHAPTER 6

Jesus Took on All Human Suffering
which He Distributes Throughout His Body

THE SUFFERING OF THE CHURCH = THE SUFFERING OF CHRIST

When Jesus suffered in his life and on the cross, he took upon himself not only all of the sins of the world but also all of the suffering of the world. Atlas had it easy: he only had to take on himself the physical weight of the globe. But Jesus took *into* himself all of the spiritual weight of all of the sins and suffering the world has ever known or ever will.

The first Adam caused our sin and suffering; the Last Adam reverses the curse and restores both holiness and health. As the New Man who is also God, Jesus is able to partake of all our suffering and cleanse us from all our sins.

Jesus's suffering was so infinite and so large that it encompasses and includes all human suffering. For Christ has come to undo all evil in us, and he transforms whatever evil he touches, including the evil of suffering, into good. He is the true King Midas who transforms evil into good and the true alchemist who transmutes base elements into those most precious.

Because of the sacramental bond between Christ and his mystical body, the church, Christ partakes of our suffering, and we partake of his sufferings. Here is a happy, if incredible truth: *the suffering of the church equals the suffering of Christ.*

If we are partakers of Christ's life and his suffering, then the suffering of the church is a sign that we belong to Jesus Christ. Far from suffering being a sign that God has abandoned his people; far from being a sign that God is absent or doesn't care: suffering is a sign that we are united to Jesus Christ.

Whenever Christians suffer today, Jesus suffers with them.

This is true of the church as a whole, but it's also true for the suffering of each one of you who is united to Jesus Christ. Your suffering is the suffering of Jesus Christ. Just as Paul's suffering was a sign of his apostleship, your suffering is a sign, by faith, of your belonging to Christ. You are all Saint Pauls, suffering for Christ, if you suffer for the sake of Christ. For Paul says: "For it has been granted to you that for the sake of Christ you should not only believe in him but also suffer for his sake, engaged in the same conflict that you saw I had and now hear that I still have" (Phil 1:29).

Since the suffering of the church equals the suffering of Christ, we can see that *Christ continues to offer up himself to the Father as a sacrificial offering of obedience in suffering—through us!*

This is why we suffer. With, in, and through Jesus Christ, we each offer up ourselves as living sacrifices, crucifying the old man in us.

God is, therefore, *redeeming man by man*: the Second Adam recapitulates the first Adam and lives the life man was supposed to live. United to Christ, we partake of his perfect life. United to Christ, our suffering is now a means of his redemption of us.

What a high calling God has in mind for us!

Man, therefore, is not only worthy of being redeemed but also, as Christ's body and blood, of participating in Christ's redemption. He is redeeming us *through us*, as his divine instruments of grace. He is redeeming man by man because God has now become man and, therefore, the suffering of Christ in his church is redemptive.

Suffering happens in community.

How can it be otherwise, when the misery of the fall of Adam and Eve has been shared with all humanity for millennia? And how can it be otherwise if we are united to Christ and each other? Living together as members of the body of Christ, we necessarily suffer together as the body of Christ.

Suffering happens in community because love happens in community. Love is the giving of self to another for the good of the other, and this necessarily means that love can only happen in community. And, indeed, love proceeds from *the Community*, the Holy Trinity, the Father, the Son, and the Holy Spirit, among whom perfect love reigns.

We are, therefore, created for community because we are created for love.

When we suffer, we suffer *as a body*, not merely as individuals.

The church, therefore, suffers as a body, the body of Jesus Christ, and this means that we always suffer together. From this truth arises the commandment to "Rejoice with those who rejoice, and weep with those who weep" (Rom 12:15). Paul's litany of sufferings, which he enumerates in 2 Corinthians 11, may seem to be his individual sufferings, but they are all endured for the sake of the churches. Because suffering happens in community, Saint Paul writes: "Who is weak, and I am not weak? Who is made to stumble, and I do not burn with indignation?" (2 Cor 11:29).

We suffer not only *as* the body of Christ but also *in* the body of Christ. Sometimes (perhaps most commonly), the ones that cause us the most suffering are not those from without but those from within: "our own familiar friends."

Saint Paul frequently speaks of those who have caused his suffering. Many of his trials and persecutions come from those who are not Christians. But he spends more time in his letters talking about those within the church who hurt the body: false apostles, false prophets, apostates, and wolves in sheep's clothing.

For every Judas who betrays Christ completely, there are eleven others who wound his body in other ways.

Why does the body of Christ turn on itself so often? Why do we hurt each other?

Because as brothers and sisters in Christ, with God as our Father, we are a family of sinners. And to live closely together as a family involves not only greater pleasure and treasure but also the risk of greater pain. If you think of your own family, you know just how much you can all hurt one another—even when those injuries are not the consequence of malice toward one another. We have only to think of divorce to be reminded of how much family can hurt family. It's no different in the body of Christ.

Sometimes, the human body turns on itself, as with autoimmune diseases, and sometimes a family turns on itself. Such is the risk of living as a family; such is the risk of living in love.

JESUS'S SUFFERING IS DISTRIBUTED THROUGHOUT HIS WHOLE BODY

If Jesus has taken on all human suffering, a suffering which he shares with his body, and if the suffering of Christ equals the suffering of his body, then we should be able to say as well that the church is suffering on behalf of all men. Since our suffering is united to Christ's and partakes of his, then the suffering of Christians has a part to play in God's redemption.

Now that Jesus paid the penalty and price for all sins and suffered all things for our sakes, we might imagine that suffering would simply vanish. And yet we sadly know that this is not the case. If Jesus is united to his body, would it make sense that while we still suffer, Jesus stands aloof from it, unable or unwilling to be a partaker of our sufferings? Jesus and his body suffer together.

The suffering of Jesus Christ which he shares with his body is distributed throughout his body. Each Christian bears not only a splinter of the true cross but, to use another image, a holographic shard of his entire suffering for humanity.

The redemptive suffering of Christ, therefore, is not confined to the final pages of the four canonical Gospels but is being written in the lives of Christians today and in every age. The glory of Christ's redemptive suffering is not hidden in some undecipherable ancient text, safely removed upon some distant shelf: it is manifest for all the world to see in Christ's power to transform the suffering of the members of his body. That which God accomplished upon the cross, he continues to accomplish through us today!

Each of our individual sufferings is connected not only to Jesus's sufferings but also to the sufferings of our brothers and sisters in Christ. As Saint Peter writes:

> Resist him, steadfast in the faith, knowing that the same sufferings are experienced by your brotherhood in the world. But may the God of all grace, who called us to His eternal glory by Christ Jesus, after you have suffered a while, perfect, establish, strengthen, and settle you. To Him be the glory and the dominion forever and ever. Amen. (1 Pet 5:9–11)

We suffer all together in ways we can scarcely imagine. It is even possible, though impossible to prove, that one of the reasons some who are saintlier suffer more than some who deserve a greater share of suffering is because they are actually helping to bear the cross of another. As Christians, we partake of each other's lives in ways far beyond our abilities to imagine.

So united is the body of Christ, that we must all wait for one another to be finally resurrected. Those who have gone before us to be with the Lord are still waiting for their resurrected bodies. This unity in Christ, of which we have been speaking, is one of the reasons why we are not reunited with our bodies until the general resurrection. The whole body of Christ will be resurrected together when he returns for his bride.

The crosses that we all bear, united as they are to the cross of Christ, demonstrate that each of our individual sufferings is, in reality, inseparable from the suffering of our brothers and sisters. If someone pokes you in the eye, the entire body feels it and responds with anguish.

The sum of all of the sufferings of every Christian who has ever lived or ever will is summed up in the sufferings of Christ, which is an immensity. We should not, however, imagine that our own individual sufferings are, therefore, unimportant. Jesus has constructed for each of us exactly the size and shape of cross he desires for us to have. He has given to each of you a splinter of his cross which he wants you to bear with and for him.

Each Christian, therefore, is a Simon of Cyrene, to whom Jesus has given a share in his cross. This might seem a cruelty, but (remembering our entire thesis about suffering leading to joy and glory) it is not. For the cross he lays upon each of us Simons unites us to Jesus and makes us bearers not only of Christ's cross but also of Christ himself.

FILLING UP WHAT IS LACKING IN CHRIST'S AFFLICTIONS

One of the most curious and incredible verses in the entire Bible is this: "Now I rejoice in my sufferings for your sake, and in my flesh I am filling up what is lacking in Christ's afflictions for the sake of his body, that is, the church" (Col 1:24).

When Saint Paul says that he is filling up what is lacking in Christ's affliction for his body, the church, he appears to border on heresy. How can Christ or his suffering lack anything? Wouldn't this make the sacrifice of Christ on the cross (and in his whole life) insufficient?

Christ's work is sufficient, but it is not yet complete, for if it were so, all suffering, sin, and death would have already passed away. Christ's work is sufficient, but something is lacking or missing because he is still in the process of conquering all of his enemies.

What is lacking, surprisingly but ecstatically, is *us, the mystical body of Christ!*

Christ's suffering is shared with his entire body, the church. But the whole church, in human history at least, has not yet come into existence. All of the suffering of Christ, which he joyfully shares with men, is still in the process of being filled up as God keeps adding saints to the world.

Never think that your suffering, no matter how trivial it seems, doesn't count. Every one of your sufferings is a part of Christ and his suffering. Every particle of your suffering is filling up what is "lacking" in Christ's afflictions, as we await our final glory.

Many Christians sadly believe that their suffering doesn't count—that somehow the only suffering that "counts" is the suffering of those who are overtly persecuted for Christ's sake. Too often, we make the mistake of envy or comparing ourselves with the colossal sufferings of Jesus. St. Paul, or the martyrs.

But Christ has come to redeem *all* of our suffering, and *all* of our suffering is united to Christ by his suffering.

There is no suffering so small that it doesn't count. All Christian suffering counts and is being redeemed by Christ!

Every form of affliction, deprivation, and humiliation counts and is, for the Christian united to Christ, a filling up of Christ's afflictions and a participation in his redemptive suffering. Every source of concern or hurt in your life *counts*: all difficulties with job, finances, children, relationships, loved ones who are self-destructing, physical pain or sickness, mental anguish or confusion, heartbreak, loss, disappointments, broken dreams, apparently wasted labor, lack of progress, hunger, thirst, insomnia, addictions, physical ugliness, scorn, ridicule, slight, insult, persecution, exclusion, gossip, slander, threat, extortion, depression, doubt, despair, hopelessness, anxiety, worry, loss of bodily functions, loss of prestige or position, etc. *All of your suffering counts, if you are a Christian, for it all matters to Jesus and is united to his sufferings for the redemption of the world.*

There is no form or size of suffering for which Christ did not come to live, suffer, and die. Your suffering matters. The personal nature of our suffering with Christ and him suffering through us is even more evident in Moffatt's translation of Colossians 1:24, which reads: "I would make up the full sum of all *that Christ has to suffer in my person* on behalf of the church, his body" (italics added).

Just how closely Christ's suffering is united to ours, and even lived out through ours, is well-expressed by Henri de Lubac when he summarizes Origen's teachings in this way: "Every day, he offers his face to spitting and his back to the whip. Every day, he is crowned with thorns. And when any member of the church is injured, it is still he who is struck in the face . . . The cry of the Lord on the cross represented our own suffering."[17]

Furthermore, all of your suffering is redeemable. How could it be otherwise? Suffering remains suffering, but remember how we've said that God takes evil and turns it into good. Remember the lesson of the cross, which is at the same time the worst thing man has ever done and the best thing God has ever done.

Here is what N. T. Wright has said about your life (including, by implication, your suffering):

> What you do for the Lord is not in vain. You are not oiling the wheels of a machine that's about to roll over a cliff. You are not restoring a great painting that's shortly going to be thrown on the fire. You are not planting roses in a garden that's about to be dug up for a building site. You are—strange as though it may seem, almost as hard to believe as the resurrection itself—accomplishing something that will become in due course part of God's new world. Every act of love, gratitude, and kindness; every work of art or music inspired by the love of God and delight in the beauty of his creation; every minute spent teaching a severely handicapped child to read or to walk; every act of care and nurture, of comfort and support, for one's fellow human beings and for that matter one's fellow nonhuman creatures; and of course every prayer, all Spirit-led teaching, every deed that spreads the gospel, builds up the church, embraces and embodies holiness rather than corruption, and makes the name of Jesus honored in the world—all of this will find its way, through the resurrecting power of God, into the new creation that God will one day make.[18]

All your labors and all your love will find its way into the New Creation, which is Christ.

All of your suffering is united to Jesus and his suffering and is, therefore, redeemable. God is the original ecologist, for he wastes nothing that

---

17. Lubac, *History and Spirit*, 237–38.
18. Wright, *Surprised by Hope*, 208.

he has made and has said, regarding the fragments from the feeding of the five thousand, "Let nothing be wasted" (John 6:12). The Lord who told his disciples to pick up the crumbs when he had just made enough bread for five thousand men will not allow a single prayer or labor of love of ours go to waste. Are you not of much more worth than crumbs from a meal?

In gathering up the fragments from the five thousand, the Good Shepherd is really gathering up the lost sheep of Israel. In the same way, the feeding of the five thousand is not really about bread but about Jesus, and it's not really about fragments of food: it's about Christ and us.

God will not let anything be wasted. Even your suffering is something God is using to redeem mankind.

Heavenly Father, You created me and most lovingly care for me. I accept all my sufferings most willingly, and as a truly obedient child I resign myself to your holy will. Grant me the strength to accept generously your loving visitation, and never let me grieve your faithful heart by giving in to impatience and discouragement. Lord Jesus, for love of You, I desire to suffer all things because for love of me You endured such cruel torments. Jesus, I unite my pains with the ones which You suffered, and I make an offering of them to the Father. O Jesus, out of the abundance of your divine goodness, give me the virtues of meekness and patience, so that I may willingly carry my cross after You. Amen. (Anonymous)

THE SECOND CUP, PART III

Christian Suffering Unites Us to Jesus Christ and, therefore, Brings Us Glory and Joy

CHAPTER 1

God Commands and Promises Glory and Joy through Suffering

THE BIBLE IS THE GREATEST BOOK ABOUT SUFFERING

While the New Testament is filled with the theology of the gospel of suffering, the Old Testament is, in a way, a history of human suffering that has resulted from man's fall. A partial list includes estrangement from God, family, and the creation (Adam and Eve in Genesis 3); jealousy, murder, brother turned against brother, and the death of a child (Cain and Abel in Genesis 4); barrenness (Sarah, Rachel, Rebekah, and Hannah); loneliness and abandonment (frequently in the Psalms); desperate longing for home (Israel in Egypt, Psalm 137); mockery and ridicule of men (Noah, Job, and Jeremiah); physical distress (Job); conquering and persecution by enemies (Israel); and every imaginable form of suffering.

But the Bible does more than chronicle the history of human suffering: in his word, God loudly proclaims the gospel of suffering—that Christian suffering united to Christ produces glory and joy for the people of God.

God's outrageous and audacious commandment to be joyful in suffering must be possible to keep. We can keep this commandment only because of the blessed presence of Jesus in every speck, iota, jot, and tittle of our suffering. Let us turn now to these outrageous and audacious commandments, as well as the many other places where the Scriptures incarnate glory and joy into the suffering of God's people.[1]

GOD COMMANDS US TO BE JOYFUL IN SUFFERING

Let us now gaze intently at those verses of the Scriptures where God commands us to be joyful. Before we begin, it seems appropriate to say a word about joy, a most misunderstood virtue.

Is joy the same as happiness or not?

On the one hand, it can't be because, while we know happiness swings more wildly than a Coney Island roller coaster with loose bolts, we know that joy is constant. On the other hand, joy, in our experience, and in the Scriptures, certainly seems a lot like happiness.

Joy is, indeed, happiness, but it is happiness unlike any other. It's like other happiness in that it creates fulfillment, satisfaction, and delight to those who have it. But it's unlike every other happiness in this one important way: while every other happiness has an earthly and finite source, joy alone is eternal and ever-present because its object and source are God.

Although joy is a commandment that God enables us to keep, it is not true that if only we truly had faith, all suffering and sorrow would vanish. Joy and sorrow can inhabit one soul at the same time. It's entirely possible, for example, to be very sorrowful for the death of a loved one and yet rejoice that he or she is with the Lord in a more blessed way.

Let us turn to see what God says in his word about the joy and glory that come through suffering. The New Testament, especially, is so engorged with verses which speak of joy and glory incarnated in the suffering of Christ's body that it's amazing that so many Christians never see it. This theme—that *the suffering of Christ's body is the means by which it receives joy and glory*—is present in virtually every epistle of the New Testament, and is a major theme in several of them. And yet this gospel of suffering, as we have been calling it, remains hidden.

---

1. For those who may be in some doubt about the things we've been saying concerning the gospel of suffering, I suggest an experiment in holy reading. The challenge is to read through all of the New Testament epistles and note the breadth and depth of times that suffering in the life of the church and apostles is mentioned. Suffering is not a minor theme in the Holy Scriptures: it's at the epicenter of God's plan of salvation, for the Father sent his Son into the world to suffer and die for the sins of the world that by his resurrection he might restore all things.

God Commands and Promises Glory and Joy through Suffering

The challenge is not to find verses and passages that illuminate this theme but to leave out even a portion of this happiest of truths.

We will repeatedly find, if we meditate on the New Testament especially, that *God commands joy in suffering but, in return, promises glory in suffering.*

Let us turn, first, to God's commandment to rejoice. We will limit ourselves to one passage where God commands joy amid suffering (two additional reflections are found in the appendix).

JOY IN SUFFERING IN 1 PETER 4:12–19

> Beloved, do not think it strange concerning the fiery trial which is to try you, as though some strange thing happened to you; but rejoice to the extent that you partake of Christ's sufferings, that when His glory is revealed, you may also be glad with exceeding joy. If you are reproached for the name of Christ, blessed are you, for the Spirit of glory and of God rests upon you. On their part He is blasphemed, but on your part He is glorified. But let none of you suffer as a murderer, a thief, an evildoer, or as a busybody in other people's matters. Yet if anyone suffers as a Christian, let him not be ashamed, but let him glorify God in this matter.
>
> For the time has come for judgment to begin at the house of God; and if it begins with us first, what will be the end of those who do not obey the gospel of God? Now
>
> "If the righteous one is scarcely saved,
> Where will the ungodly and the sinner appear?"
>
> Therefore let those who suffer according to the will of God commit their souls to Him in doing good, as to a faithful Creator.
> (1 Pet 4:12–19)

Peter's first letter, in its entirety, may be seen as a gospel of suffering, for this theme appears in every chapter of the book. In the passage at hand, Peter makes the assumption, first made by his Lord and also by his fellow inspired epistle writers, that Christians will suffer or endure "fiery trials."

Suffering is not something strange to Christians: it is common, in every sense of that word. Peter, like his Master, commands us (it's really God doing the commanding, of course) to rejoice in our sufferings. The reason is at the heart of the meditation of this book on suffering: that our suffering is a sharing in Christ's suffering. Nothing less can make suffering not only bearable but, more astonishingly, also a cause for rejoicing.

How much more plainly could the Spirit say this mysterious truth to us—that we should rejoice when things hurt us because such pain is a participation in the sufferings of Christ? And if it is true that our suffering is a share in Christ's suffering, then joy must be part of our response to it. There is a future glory implied by what Peter proclaims, but at least some of the joy and glory must already be present with us, or else Christ is robbed of his power and glory in us.

Peter continues in a more specific manner, turning next to the idea of being insulted for the name of Christ. While this being insulted for the name of Christ seems to have special reference to an explicit displaying of Christ's name and an explicit insult in return, a more general promise is also implied. Is it not possible that every kind of insult we bear—if we accept it for Christ's sake—falls under this promise of blessing? Must we wait for explicit persecution to receive a share in Christ's suffering and, therefore, his glory and joy?

The same may be said of Peter's statement that "if anyone suffers as a Christian, let him not be ashamed, but let him glorify God in this matter" (v. 16). That is, *any* suffering that we receive *as the suffering of Christ* is something that will bring God glory. Likewise, with Peter's teaching in verse 19 that "Therefore let those who suffer according to the will of God commit their souls to Him in doing good." Any suffering that we experience that is not the result of our own sinfulness is a suffering according to the will of God, *if we commit this suffering to God as a share in the sufferings of Christ*.

GOD PROMISES US GLORY IN SUFFERING

While direct commandments to rejoice in suffering are not common in the New Testament, examples where glory and joy are promised through suffering are quite numerous, especially when we consider all equivalent words and concepts for "glory," "joy," and "suffering."[2] We will look at one

---

2. A list of passages where joy and glory are set in the context of suffering in the New Testament includes the following: Matt 5:11–12; Luke 17:24, 25; 24:26; John 16:20–22; John 17:1–5; Acts 5:41; 16:25; Rom 5:3–5; 6:3–5; 8:18–30; 1 Cor 12:12; 2 Cor 1:3–7; 4:7–18; 7:4–10; 8:1–2; Eph 3:13; Phil 1:20–30; 2:5–11, 17–18; 3:10–11, 21; Col 1:18–24; 1 Thess 2:14–20; 2 Tim 1:8–12; 2:3–13; Heb 2:9–11; 4:15–16; 10:34; 12:2; Jas 1:2–4, 12; 5:10–11; and 1 Pet 1:6–11; 3:14–18; 4:13–19; 5:1, 5–6, 9–10.

A survey of the theme of humiliation to exaltation, a variation on the gospel of

passage where God promises us glory from our suffering (two additional reflections are found in the appendix).

2 CORINTHIANS 4:7–18

The gospel of suffering is illuminated in 2 Corinthians 4:7–11.[3]

> But we have this treasure in jars of clay, to show that the surpassing power belongs to God and not to us. We are afflicted in every way, but not crushed; perplexed, but not driven to despair; persecuted, but not forsaken; struck down, but not destroyed; *always carrying in the body the death of Jesus, so that the life of Jesus may also be manifested in our bodies.* For we who live are always being given over to death for Jesus' sake, so *that the life of Jesus also may be manifested in our mortal flesh*. So death is at work in us, but life in you. And since we have the same spirit of faith, according to what is written, "I believed and therefore I spoke," we also believe and therefore speak, knowing that He who raised up the Lord Jesus will also raise us up with Jesus, and will present us with you. For all things are for your sakes, that grace, having spread through the many, may cause thanksgiving to abound to the glory of God. Therefore we do not lose heart. Even though our *outward man is perishing, yet the inward man is being renewed day by day. For our light affliction, which is but for a moment, is working for us a far more exceeding and eternal weight of glory*, while we do not look at the things which are seen, but at the things which are not seen. For the things which are seen are temporary, but the things which are not seen are eternal. (Italics added)

The immediate context of 2 Corinthians 4 is 2 Corinthians 3, where Saint Paul compares the glory of the old and new covenants. So glorious was the old covenant that when Moses came down from being with God, his face shone so luminously that he had to wear a veil before the children of Israel. By contrast, the glory of the new covenant in Christ is much more glorious, and we see God without veils.

The unbelievably good news at the end of 2 Corinthians 3 is this: that the glory of the Lord is no longer merely reflected off the face of one man but now inheres in the entire body of Christ, which is being transformed

---

suffering, would yield an even lengthier list.

3. Much of the entire letter of 2 Corinthians deals with Paul's sufferings in union with his Lord.

into the same image from glory to glory! The glory of the Lord that was manifest at Mount Sinai and which was reflected on the face of Moses now resides in us, through the work of the Spirit as he transforms us into the temple of the Lord![4]

After exclaiming in 2 Corinthians 3 about the glory of God which he has shone on us through Christ, Paul reverts in chapter 4 to the notion of hiddenness and invisibility. This hiddenness of God's glory is a crucial point if we are to believe that suffering leads to glory. Although the glory of the new covenant far surpasses that of the old, its glory is of a different nature. The ministry of death of the old covenant was written on stone, but the ministry of life in the new is written on our hearts. Likewise, the glory of the old covenant was made manifest by tangible, physical sensations: thunder and lightning, the voice of many waters, and Moses's shining face. But the glory of the new, which far surpasses the old, is actually *less visible* to the natural senses.

This hidden glory of the new covenant is a common experience and source of frustration for Christians. For the miracle of the Eucharist is not as easily seen as the miracle of the manna or the feeding of the five thousand. The body of Christ, which is the church, is not as easy to point to as the natural body of Christ that traversed the mountains and valleys of Israel.

Where has the glory of God gone? Should the church have cried "Ichabod!" for the past two millennia? Saint Paul assures us that the glory of the Lord is now far greater than before, but it comes to us in a different way, which by now you should have been able to guess. The glory of the Lord in the new covenant comes by God becoming a man, by God hiding himself in a tiny earthen vessel in Bethlehem. The glory of the Lord comes riding lowly on a donkey. It comes especially on Mount Calvary, when the King of Glory is lifted up on the cross of shame and humiliation.

Where has the glory of the Lord gone after the resurrection and ascension? Paul tells us that it has gone into the earthen vessels of the church. The

---

4. This glory, however, is still veiled, but in a different manner. It is now veiled, Paul teaches in the beginning of 2 Corinthians 4, to those who are not in Christ: "But even if our gospel is veiled, it is veiled to those who are perishing, whose minds the god of this age has blinded, who do not believe, lest the light of the gospel of the glory of Christ, who is the image of God, should shine on them" (vv. 3–4). Unbelievers can't see this glory, however. One of the reasons (as we'll see) is that unbelievers can't see how suffering could lead to glory or be a sign of God and His blessed presence. For Christians, on the other hand, God "has shone in our hearts to give the light of the knowledge of the glory of God in the face of Jesus Christ" (v. 6).

God who once spoke through lightning and thunder, fire and flood, and manna and water, became the creation and spoke through the Incarnate Son. But that same Son who once spoke in his natural body now speaks through his mystical body, the church. The same God who first humbled himself to become man in the person of Christ now humbles himself to become man in the person of Christ in his mystical body.

Where has the glory of the Lord gone? The incredible answer is "into us"!

Though this should not surprise us as Christians, it nevertheless does. The God who made Mary his dwelling place now makes us his dwelling place as well. The God who suffered for us by giving up all for us continues to humble himself and even humiliate himself by dwelling in the church.

The glory of God in pulling off such an improbable miracle is so audacious and unexpected that laughter is not an inappropriate response.

We have this treasure in earthen vessels, which is Christ in us, the glory of the Father, so "that the excellence of the power may be of God and not of us" (v. 7). And yet, united to Christ, we have this treasure in earthen vessels that when we humble ourselves with Christ, we might partake of his glory. We have this treasure in these earthen vessels so that even as we are humbled, God is exalted.

This treasure in earthen vessels is Christ in us. But it is the entire Christ, for as we have been saying, we can't separate the life from the death of Christ any more than we can separate his cross from his resurrection. The glory of God is to humble and hide himself in these earthen vessels. The glory of man is to humbly receive our Lord, as Mary did before us, knowing that we are not worthy that he should enter into the houses of our bodies.

These earthen vessels house the whole Christ, and so Paul says that we are "always carrying about in the body the dying of the Lord Jesus, that the life of Jesus also may be manifested in our body" (v. 10). Paul expresses this in a very personal way in his letters. He, Paul, is dying and subject to death, to bring life to the churches of Christ. This is at least part of what he means when he continues in verse 11 by saying: "For we who live are always delivered to death for Jesus's sake, that the life of Jesus also may be manifested in our mortal flesh."

But Paul's overall point is broader. Paul is an imitator and partaker of Christ: he is a type of all Christians who are continually giving up their lives to Christ that they might truly live. He's not throwing a pity party or a proud party, saying, "Look at me," either for how terrible things are for him or for how great he is for suffering so much. Paul sees himself as a partaker of Christ and an exemplar for those in the churches entrusted to his care. Paul is another Christ, offering up his life so that those in Corinth might live (v. 12).

This glory then, which is Christ in us, is manifested in our suffering, as we become "little Christs," humble ourselves before the Lord, and offer up our lives for the sake of others.

The gospel of suffering cannot be said more simply than this: "For our light affliction, which is but for a moment, is working for us a far more exceeding and eternal weight of glory" (v. 17).

In these few words, Saint Paul sets before us several truths. First, he contrasts the magnitude of the affliction (light) compared to the glory (far more exceeding and eternal). This is not the only place where Paul sets forth such a bold contrast inherent in the gospel of suffering. In Romans 8 Paul speaks these very similar and familiar words to us: "For I consider that the sufferings of this present time are not worthy to be compared with the glory which shall be revealed in us" (v. 18). Once again, we see that our glory to come dwarfs our present suffering in magnitude.

By this contrast, we may know the love and goodness of God; by this contrast, we may find strength to endure and even rejoice in this life.

This surpassing glory and joy of the life to come, vis-à-vis our present suffering, is true both in terms of intensity and duration. The glory that shall be ours far exceeds the suffering we now endure. But the glory is also eternal, while the suffering is for a century at most, and usually less.

But Paul is saying something more here in 2 Corinthians 4 than he says in Romans 8, for he not only proclaims this blessed contrast but also reveals a mysterious, inner synergy between our suffering and the glory. Paul is *not* saying: "This life is all suffering, but even though it is, the future life will be all glorious, and its glory will outweigh the suffering of this life." He's saying something much more incarnational and, therefore, something that is of even greater comfort and import to those who suffer in this life.

What Paul actually says is that "our light affliction, which is but for a moment, *is working for us* a far more exceeding and eternal weight of glory." In other words, our suffering is actually a means of manifesting or producing this glory. The light affliction of this life is producing in us the far more exceeding and eternal weight of glory. The glory of which we partake, which is Christ's glory and not our own, is something in which we already participate. Having been baptized into Christ, we get the whole Christ: both crucifixion and resurrection; both death and life; both suffering and glory.

Once again, we see in the gospel of suffering that while there is a temporal progression, first the suffering and then the glory, there is also a union of suffering and glory in this life, as was true for Jesus. The cross of Christ was not only his ultimate suffering but *also* his being lifted up in glory. The suffering of the Christian, therefore, already truly partakes of the glory of Christ but is also a sign of the glory to come. The fullness, that greater and more blessed magnitude of glory and joy, is still in the future. But that future is a future which is not disconnected from our present.

> *My soul doth magnify the Lord,*
> *And my spirit hath rejoiced in God my Saviour.*
> *For he hath regarded the low estate of his handmaiden: for, behold, from henceforth all generations shall call me blessed.*
> *For he that is mighty hath done to me great things; and holy is his name.*
> *And his mercy is on them that fear him from generation to generation.*
> *He hath shewed strength with his arm; he hath scattered the proud in the imagination of their hearts.*
> *He hath put down the mighty from their seats, and exalted them of low degree.*
> *He hath filled the hungry with good things; and the rich he hath sent empty away.*
> *He hath helped his servant Israel, in remembrance of his mercy;*
> *As he spake to our fathers, to Abraham, and to his seed for ever. Amen.*
> (Luke 1:46–55, KJV)

CHAPTER 2

Suffering Unites Us to the Source of All Joy

We've been discussing the gospel of suffering and how God transforms our suffering into glory and joy. We've meditated on how Jesus, by his incarnation and life of suffering, took the cup for us and how, as a result, he has sanctified even suffering. What fallen creatures mean for evil and what causes suffering, God means for good and transforms into our glory and joy.

We've marveled, as well, at how Jesus, by his incarnation, shares his whole life with us: His death and life, and his suffering and glory. Because of this, suffering has become a means by which we are united to Christ, having been baptized into his death and resurrection.

The Scriptures, we rediscover, teach this gospel of suffering, that God both commands and promises us glory and joy through suffering with Christ.

And now it's time to exult in a litany of reasons why we rejoice in the midst of our sufferings. We will discuss these reasons to rejoice in our sufferings in this order over the next several chapters:

1. We rejoice because suffering unites us to the source of all joy.

2. We rejoice because we partake of Christ's victory over his enemies and ours.

3. We rejoice because we have been counted worthy to partake of God's redemption.

4. We rejoice because God is treating us as his children.
5. We rejoice because suffering unites us to one another.
6. We rejoice because we suffer for the good of others.
7. We rejoice because suffering is an angel and the world's greatest mnemonic device.
8. We rejoice because suffering transforms us into the image and character of Christ.
9. We rejoice because you can't have a resurrection without a crucifixion.
10. We rejoice because suffering is a measure of God and man.
11. We rejoice because our suffering brings glory to God.

SUFFERING UNITES US TO THE SOURCE OF ALL JOY

All Christian suffering united to Christ is intended to end in our glory and joy. We rejoice when we suffer as Christians because we are united to Jesus Christ, the source of all blessing and joy. Ponder this for a moment: if what the Scriptures say about union with Christ is true, how can this union end in anything less than glory and joy?

Jesus Christ is the beginning and the end, the Alpha and Omega, of human existence. He is its eternal destiny, a destiny which ends in glory at the right hand of the Father and concludes with joy at the Marriage Feast of the Lamb. Whenever Christians have gazed intently on Christ and beheld him, they have experienced the joy of the Lord.

Regardless of the medium which conveys us to Jesus, it brings us joy: the word of God, the people of God, the Sacraments, the creation, prayer, and, yes, even suffering and loss. Perhaps the greatest cause of suffering of all is our failure to see Jesus, though he is present, a failure by which we rob ourselves of the joy that could be ours.

And the glory? The glory, too, is always present and available, but it, too, is often hidden. It's hidden precisely because it comes incarnated in our suffering. Christ's glory was his humiliation, and so ours must be. Already, Saint Paul says, we are more than conquerors with Christ (Rom 8:37); already we are seated in the heavenly places with Jesus (Eph 2:6), and already we must rejoice.

"It is the glory of God to conceal a matter, but the glory of kings is to search out a matter" (Prov 25:2). Nowhere are we acting more like real kings and queens than when we discover glory and joy in suffering, because Christ has revealed himself to us in the midst of it.

If we truly apprehended that our suffering unites us to our Lord, we would have sufficient reason to rejoice. For what reason have we been created, other than to find union with our beloved Lord? And what is the secret prayer of every Christian soul but that it might be reunited with its beloved, from whom it has been cruelly separated?

What joy could be ours if, through suffering, we discovered the pearl of great price and the treasure of treasures that is the object of every human quest! To have the deepest, sweetest, most peaceful, and fruitful fellowship with God is worth any price, even the bargain price of our own suffering in this life.

Remembering all that we have said about Christ uniting himself to us, we rejoice because our suffering unites us to the source of all joy. *This union with Christ is the source of our every joy, including the reasons found in Chapters 3–12 for why we rejoice in our sufferings.*

> *Ah Lord God, Thou holy lover of my Soul, when Thou comest into my Soul, all that is within me shall rejoice. Thou art my Glory and the exultation of my heart. Thou art my Hope and Refuge in the day of my trouble.*
>
> *Set me free from all evil passions, and heal my heart of all inordinate affections, that being cured and thoroughly cleansed, may I be made fit to love, courageous to suffer, steady to persevere. Nothing is sweeter than love, nothing more courageous, nothing fuller or better in heaven and earth; because Love is born of God, and cannot rest but in God, above all created things.* (Thomas à Kempis)

CHAPTER 3

We Partake of Christ's Victory Over His Enemies

One of the ancient ways of understanding Christ's atonement for the sins of the world is through the theology of Christus Victor. We rejoice in Christ because of his great victory over his enemies, which are also our enemies. The Scriptures reveal an often-invisible spiritual battle in this world. Jesus was born into the front lines of this battle and fought against his enemies and ours his entire life. This is only one of the reasons that Jesus had to suffer and die.

This battle was present from the moment Herod the Great sought to murder Jesus until the day Pontius Pilate sentenced him to death. We are most conscious of this battle when Jesus was tempted by Satan in the wilderness and also in the garden of Gethsemane when Jesus was tempted to do his will and not that of the Father. But his entire life was a spiritual battle in which he confronted his enemies and conquered them.

Jesus fought and triumphed over his ancient foes, who ally themselves against Christ and his body: sin, death, and the devil. Christ is so powerful that when he touches death, death dies; when he touches sin, sin evaporates and is made clean; when he does mortal battle with the devil, Satan must flee the field; and when he touches suffering, he transforms it into a means of union with himself, which is not only the path to victory but also the place of glory and joy.

By Jesus's obedience, he conquered sin, which had enslaved us and cruelly oppressed us. This was not a single moment of victory at the cross: it was, instead, a lifetime of moment-by-moment obedience that endured his entire life. Jesus's death on the cross was only the final, perfect obedience in a life that was one continuously chosen moment of obedience to the will of the Father.

By Jesus's death and resurrection, he conquered death. By his suffering and death, Christ has defanged and killed death. By his suffering and death, Christ has transfigured death into the portal to life everlasting. When Jesus died for the sins of the world, it was not only Jesus that died but also the first and old Adam. When Jesus died, the old world order, ruled by his ancient foes, was catastrophically overthrown. Heaven invaded earth and subdued it.

Christians have been jubilant for two millennia at the victory of Christ over the grave, of which they are partakers. Here is what Saint Chrysostom says in his paschal sermon read in Orthodox churches on Pascha:

> Enjoy ye all the feast of faith: Receive ye all the riches of loving-kindness. Let no one bewail his poverty, for the universal kingdom has been revealed. Let no one weep for his iniquities, for pardon has shown forth from the grave. Let no one fear death, for the Savior's death has set us free. He that was held prisoner of it has annihilated it. By descending into Hell, He made Hell captive. He embittered it when it tasted of His flesh. And Isaiah, foretelling this, did cry: Hell, said he, was embittered, when it encountered Thee in the lower regions. It was embittered, for it was abolished. It was embittered, for it was mocked. It was embittered, for it was slain. It was embittered, for it was overthrown. It was embittered, for it was fettered in chains. It took a body, and met God face to face. It took earth, and encountered Heaven. It took that which was seen, and fell upon the unseen.
>
> O Death, where is your sting? O Hell, where is your victory? Christ is risen, and you are overthrown. Christ is risen, and the demons are fallen. Christ is risen, and the angels rejoice. Christ is risen, and life reigns. Christ is risen, and not one dead remains in the grave. For Christ, being risen from the dead, is become the first fruits of those who have fallen asleep. To Him be glory and dominion unto ages of ages. Amen.

By Jesus, the devil is unlorded and stripped naked, which causes him to flee. After Jesus's victory over Satan in the wilderness, Satan was rebuked and got behind Christ, retreating and waiting for an opportune time. The millions of battles Satan has fought over thousands of years with God and his people reached their climax at the cross.

At the Place of the Skull, the most ancient of prophecies regarding the Christ, that he would crush the head of the serpent, was fulfilled. At the crucifixion, the prince of this world was cast out and exorcised from man.

Let us return, as always, to the cross. The cross is the mountain, the place in the Bible where heaven and earth meet. God speaks decisively on this mountain, Mount Calvary, for this mountain is the mountain of God's glory, where the human Christ is lifted up in glory for all men to see. This mountain, the mountain of human suffering and shame, is also the mountain of human glory and joy.

What is this victory of Christ, which we celebrate and of which we are partakers? It is Christ's victory over the unholy trinity of sin, death, and the devil. It is our deliverance from the house of bondage to all of these things; it is the divine judgment on the enemies of God. It is the forgiveness of sins and the breaking of the power of sin and darkness over us; it is the breaking of the teeth and the arms of the ungodly in their false authority. It is the casting out of Satan from heaven; it is the reentry into the garden out of the wilderness and our ability to live a holy, obedient, and pleasing life to the Father, through the Son. It is man's reentry into paradise, with the angels who once guarded the garden and who guarded the empty tomb of Christ themselves now ushering us back in with a festal procession.

We rejoice because we have been baptized into the death and life of Jesus Christ, which together manifest for the entire cosmos the victory of God over every evil. Sin, death, and Satan, like any cruel despots, will not allow their people to go for free: a huge payment or total military victory are the only ways to free those enslaved under such evil rulers. Christ's death, therefore, may be seen both as the price of victory, as well as his total victory over his enemies.

It is both Jesus's death and his resurrection which constitute his victory over his enemies and ours. What is Christ's resurrection? It is the resurrection of the Crucified Word; it is the triumph of life over death. It is the Father's justification of the holiness of the Son, the New Man; it is his satisfaction with his Son with whom he is well pleased, and, therefore, his satisfaction with man. It is God's "Amen!" to the cross and God's everlasting "Yes" to both himself and man. It is both the promise of the eschaton, to which we will be resurrected with incorruptible, imperishable, death-free, suffering-free bodies, as well as the participation of this promise even in this life.

The resurrection is not only the coming again to life of the limp and lifeless body of Jesus: it's also the coming again to life of the limp and lifeless mystical body of Christ. In his crucifixion and resurrection, Jesus is the Tree of Life that died for us, was planted in the ground, and which multiplies and is fruitful beyond measure. He is the Seed planted in the garden, who produces in the new humanity of his body a new Tree of Life, of which the sons of the Second Adam partake. The resurrection is God the Father breathing life into the Second Adam who had returned to the dust, by the power of the Holy Spirit. It is the power of God to breathe the life of Christ by his Spirit into the mystical body of Christ on the day of Pentecost.

At the crucifixion, it was not only Christ's natural body that was smitten to death: the mystical body of believers was also struck, scattered, and found to be lifeless. But at the resurrection it was not only Christ's natural body that was brought to life but also his mystical body. For once the head resurrected, the body, by the power of the Spirit, quickly reattached itself. Once the body of Christ had risen, his members had a place to live once again.

Jesus's trial is the last judgment, prefigured. The judgment upon Christ was the judgment upon man, whose nature Christ bore. The crucifixion was the Father's "no" to man, but Jesus's resurrection is God's "yes" to man. Christ's resurrection is the justification of the Son, into whose justification we are baptized as Christians and by which we are also justified. The cross and the resurrection are the great restoration of all things, and the rectification of all that was wrong with the cosmos and especially man. The cross and the resurrection are the great reversal and ultimate plot twist, by which an upside-down world is made right-side up again.

The glory of the Glorified rubs off on those who touch him.

Just as the woman with the flow of blood touched only the hem of Jesus's garment, and he felt his virtue (or glory) flow to her, so when we touch Jesus by baptism and faith (or, rather, he touches us), we partake of his glory. The children of a king partake of his glory, even if they themselves have done nothing glorious. Even the glory of fictional kings flows to the princes and princesses of fairy tales.

And so Christians partake of the glory of the Glorified One. The glory of the Glorious One is unlike the faux glory of worldly celebrities, which never truly communicates any glory to those they touch or who seek their autographs: when the King of Glory touches us in our suffering, we partake

We Partake of Christ's Victory Over His Enemies

of him and receive an immense glory that is not ours by merit and yet truly becomes ours in Christ.

We rejoice in our sufferings because they are bound together with the sufferings and death of Jesus Christ, which also means they are bound together with his resurrection. We rejoice because we partake of Christ's victory over his enemies and ours!

> *Death, be not proud, though some have called thee*
> *Mighty and dreadful, for thou art not so;*
> *For those whom thou think'st thou dost overthrow*
> *Die not, poor Death, nor yet canst thou kill me.*
> *From rest and sleep, which but thy pictures be,*
> *Much pleasure; then from thee much more must flow,*
> *And soonest our best men with thee do go,*
> *Rest of their bones, and soul's delivery.*
> *Thou art slave to fate, chance, kings, and desperate men,*
> *And dost with poison, war, and sickness dwell,*
> *And poppy or charms can make us sleep as well*
> *And better than thy stroke; why swell'st thou then?*
> *One short sleep past, we wake eternally*
> *And death shall be no more; Death, thou shalt die.*
> (John Donne, Holy Sonnet 10)

CHAPTER 4

We have been Counted Worthy to Partake of God's Redemption

We rejoice in our sufferings because we have been counted worthy to partake of God's redemption.

When God became man in Christ, he began his mighty work of salvation by entering into the fallen condition of man from the inside. God did not just wave his magic wand, wiggle his nose, or close his eyes and blink, and magically save mankind and redeem the world. Since ruin befell the cosmos by man, by man the cosmos must be saved.

Perhaps God could have redeemed the world without employing men: it's highly significant that he chose not to. God's using man to redeem man has something to do with God's desire to make a creature in his image fit for marriage and eternal union with him.

Because Christ's redemption of the world necessarily involved his suffering and the taking on of all human suffering, and because we are truly united with him on the basis of the incarnation and through the means of faith and baptism, we, too, necessarily suffer. This suffering, united with Christ, is, therefore, redemptive in nature.

This is one of the greatest of human and, therefore, Christian hopes: that my suffering counts for something; that my suffering is not in vain; that my suffering has a good purpose and is not merely pain. United to Christ, the suffering of Christians is redemptive. To accept this requires that we might need a stronger view of what the incarnation and union with Christ entail. To accept this is the key to appropriating the glory and joy that are already ours in Christ but which are seen only weakly without a theology of suffering.

Let us say it this way: Jesus continues his work of the redemption and restoration of the world through his mystical body, the church. What he experienced as a recapitulation of the creation, fall, and redemption of humanity, the church recapitulates in her suffering and life. This is the dominant theme in Luke's Acts of the Apostles.

When Christians suffer, therefore, their suffering is the suffering of Christ, and the meaning of their suffering is the meaning of Christ's suffering: the redemption of the world.

We might, therefore, also say that not only has Christ redeemed us by his suffering, and that he is redeeming the world through our sufferings, but also that *he is also redeeming suffering itself through us!*

The apostles were keenly aware that the ministry into which they had entered was not their own but their Lord's. This is especially salient in the letters of Saint Paul, but it was also manifest in the ministry of the apostles from the day of Pentecost forward. When the Jews laid hands upon the apostles and beat them, "they departed from the presence of the council, rejoicing that they were counted worthy to suffer shame for His name" (Acts 5:41).

Notice not only how the apostles suffered for their Lord from the beginning of their ministry but also their attitude: they *"rejoiced that they were counted worthy to suffer shame for His name."* Suffering, in the ministers of Christ, resulted not in numbness or resentment *but in joy*. Their joy, in this instance, was because they knew that their sufferings were a true partaking of the sufferings and life of Christ. What they suffered was not only physical pain but also the shame that came with a public "trial" and humiliation before men. In this, they were made like their Lord. In this, they partook of Christ's ministry of redemption.

When the apostles rejoiced to suffer for Jesus in the first century, they did not do so as a badge of human merit or as a test of their endurance in Christ. The suffering in the life of the apostles was a genuine sign that they belonged to Jesus Christ. Having been justified with Christ in their sufferings, they rejoiced to be united with the source of all joy.

Paul's ministry was conceived with a promise from Jesus that his ministry would be a ministry of suffering for Christ. Jesus told Ananias: "Go, for he is a chosen vessel of Mine to bear My name before Gentiles, kings, and the children of Israel. For I will show him how many things he must suffer for My name's sake" (Acts 9:15–16).

Throughout his epistles, but especially in his letters to the church in Corinth, Saint Paul proclaims his belonging to Christ in terms of his suffering.

Paul begins his second letter to the church at Corinth with a discussion of suffering, and the entire letter is framed as a defense of Paul's apostolic ministry, primarily in terms of what Paul has suffered for his Lord by suffering for the body of Christ. This is a grand irony, for when Jesus confronted Saul on the road to Damascus, He asked him: "Saul, Saul, why are you persecuting *Me*?" From that very moment, Paul understood Jesus and his ministry in terms of suffering. The irony is that when Paul became an apostle, a representative of Jesus Christ, Paul suffered for Christ *by* his suffering for the body of Christ.

Saint Paul certainly believed that his suffering was a true participation in and manifestation of the death and life of Jesus. He says in 2 Corinthians 4 that he is: "always carrying about in the body the dying of the Lord Jesus, that the life of Jesus also may be manifested in our body. For we who live are always delivered to death for Jesus' sake, that the life of Jesus also may be manifested in our mortal flesh" (vv. 10–11).

Paul's ministry for God is a ministry of suffering for Christ by suffering for Christ's body. He writes in 2 Corinthians 6:

> But in all things we commend ourselves as ministers of God: in much patience, in tribulations, in needs, in distresses, in stripes, in imprisonments, in tumults, in labors, in sleeplessness, in fastings; by purity, by knowledge, by longsuffering, by kindness, by the Holy Spirit, by sincere love, by the word of truth, by the power of God, by the armor of righteousness on the right hand and on the left, by honor and dishonor, by evil report and good report; as deceivers, and yet true; as unknown, and yet well known; as dying, and behold we live; as chastened, and yet not killed; as sorrowful, yet always rejoicing; as poor, yet making many rich; as having nothing, and yet possessing all things. (vv. 4–10)

In this passage, Paul is a minister of God, *precisely in his sufferings*. Of particular note are verses 9 and 10: "as dying, and behold we live; as chastened, and yet not killed; as sorrowful, yet always rejoicing; as poor, yet making many rich; as having nothing, and *yet* possessing all things." The theme of life in death is manifest here, as well as the theme of joy in the midst of suffering: "as sorrowful, yet always rejoicing." Christ's self-emptying is also present, for Paul is rich in his poverty and possesses all things, even though he's given up all for Christ.

Paul repeats the same theme in even greater detail in 2 Corinthians 11, putting his litany of suffering in the context of Christ's ministry: "Are they ministers of Christ?—I speak as a fool—I am more: in labors more abundant, in stripes above measure, in prisons more frequently, in deaths often" (vv. 23–29).

Paul, like his Lord, emptied himself of his glory for the good of others. He has willingly endured the loss of all things (which is the essence of suffering) for the sake of gaining Christ, who was Paul's eternal glory and joy.

The same theme is expressed by Paul in his letter to the church in Philippi.

> But what things were gain to me, these I have counted loss for Christ. Yet indeed I also count all things loss for the excellence of the knowledge of Christ Jesus my Lord, for whom I have suffered the loss of all things, and count them as rubbish, that I may gain Christ and be found in Him, not having my own righteousness, which *is* from the law, but that which *is* through faith in Christ, the righteousness which is from God by faith; that I may know Him and the power of His resurrection, and the fellowship of His sufferings, being conformed to His death, if, by any means, I may attain to the resurrection from the dead (Phil 3:7–11).

Paul's life, including his necessary suffering, was a participation in and revelation of the death and resurrection of Paul's Lord. Paul's suffering was a sign that he was an apostle, a minister of Christ who represented Christ, one sent to proclaim the death and resurrection of Christ *in his body*.

And so my suffering as a Christian is the result of my sin and the fallenness of the creation and also a means by which God redeems me and the world.

Our suffering, therefore, has a double meaning. When Joseph was sold into slavery by his own familiar brothers, they meant it for evil, but God meant it for good, for the salvation of his people. When Jesus was crucified by both Roman and Jew, it was the worst thing man could ever do but the best thing that God has ever done. While my suffering itself remains an evil, God has now, through Christ, transformed it into a means of his redemption of the world.

As Pope Paul II has said: "Every man has *his own share in the redemption*. Each one is also *called to share in that suffering* through which the redemption has been accomplished. . . . In bringing about the redemption through suffering, Christ *has* also *raised human suffering to the level of redemption*.[5]

The Pope also wrote: "Those who share in the sufferings of Christ preserve in their own sufferings a very special particle of the infinite treasure of the world's redemption, and can share this treasure with others."[6]

We rejoice because every time we suffer for Christ, we, like Christ, beat down Satan under our feet on Golgotha. Every time we obey the Father, the Son, through us, undoes the ancient curse: taking dominion over evil by the good things He does through us; taking dominion over sin by His obedience in and through us; and taking dominion over death by living in and through us.

We rejoice because we are counted worthy to suffer for Christ's sake. I rejoice to suffer for You, my Christ!

> *Worthy is the Lamb who was slain,*
> *to receive power and wealth and wisdom and might*
> *and honor and glory and blessing!*
> *I am not worthy to untie the latchet of Your sandals;*
> *I am not worthy that You should enter my house;*
> *I am not worthy to partake of the crumbs from under Your table.*
>
> *Yet make me worthy, O Worthy of worthies,*
> *and, having made me worthy of You and pleasing in Your sight,*
> *count me worthy of suffering for Your Name,*
> *as You suffered first for me.*
>
> *To Him who sits on the throne and to the Lamb*
> *be blessing and honor and glory and might forever and ever!*

---

5. John Paul II, *Christian Meaning of Human Suffering*, 52–53. The italics are the Pope's.

6. John Paul II, *Christian Meaning of Human Suffering*, 77–78.

CHAPTER 5

God is Treating Us as His Children

We rejoice because our suffering means God is treating us as his children.

Christian suffering, therefore, is not random pain. Just as we see the face of Jesus in suffering, so, in the hands of the Good Shepherd, suffering leads us safely to God. Suffering is the means by which we are continually brought back to the Shepherd when we wander like sheep from him. What feels like punishment is, in fact, discipline.

The writer of Hebrews explains God's intentions in allowing us to feel pain:

> My son, do not despise the chastening of the Lord,
> Nor be discouraged when you are rebuked by Him;
> For whom the Lord loves He chastens,
> And scourges every son whom He receives.

> If you endure chastening, God deals with you as with sons; for what son is there whom a father does not chasten? But if you are without chastening, of which all have become partakers, then you are illegitimate and not sons. Furthermore, we have had human fathers who corrected us, and we paid them respect. Shall we not much more readily be in subjection to the Father of spirits and live? For they indeed for a few days chastened us as seemed best to them, but He for our profit, that we may be partakers of His holiness. Now no chastening seems to be joyful for the present, but painful; nevertheless, afterward it yields the peaceable fruit of righteousness to those who have been trained by it. (12:5–11)

The Second Cup, Part III

God chastens, or disciplines, his children. We are so accustomed to thinking parental discipline to be a negative thing that we've lost the true value of it. Parental discipline partakes of the gospel of suffering: what seems like pain inflicted by an angry parent is actually meant for good by a loving parent. God disciplines his children, for discipline in the Bible is instruction in wisdom and holiness. And it is *bodily* in nature.

What's most shocking about God's discipline is that he did not spare his own Son. God disciplines every son whom he receives, including the scourged and suffering Son. The writer of Hebrews teaches that Jesus "who, in the days of His flesh, when He had offered up prayers and supplications, with vehement cries and tears to Him who was able to save Him from death, and was heard because of His godly fear, though He was a Son, yet *He learned obedience by the things which He suffered*" (Heb 12:7–8).

Two things are remarkable about this passage. First is the idea that Jesus actually had to *learn* obedience. We sometimes naively assume that Jesus, in his humanity, automatically knew all things, including how to obey. But if he was truly human, then, like us, he had to *grow* in wisdom and stature (Luke 2:52). When Jesus was a child, he subjected himself to the parental discipline of Joseph and Mary (Luke 2:51). Even more scandalous is this truth: Jesus learned obedience to his Heavenly Father by what he suffered. If Christ in his humanity learned obedience by what he suffered, then we who are baptized into Christ must also learn obedience by what we suffer.

The Father disciplined the Son for us. In this, God the Father proves himself more perfect and loving than King David, for we read, in a chilling verse from 1 Kings 1:6 concerning David and Absalom: "His father had never at any time displeased him by asking, 'Why have you done thus and so?'" (ESV).

David, who disciplined himself, his troops, and his enemies, did not discipline or displease his sons. As a result, Absalom tried to usurp David's throne and commit patricide and regicide; Amnon raped Absalom's sister, Tamar, while David took no action in response; and Adonijah also tried to seize the throne after David's death. Because David never caused his sons to suffer with godly discipline and good intent, his sons caused David and others to suffer from their evil. Undisciplined children attempt to usurp both God and parent.

God disciplines his children so that they may be truly his children. He disciplines us "for our profit, that we may be partakers of His holiness"

God is Treating Us as His Children

(Heb 12:10). Here is another disguised form of the gospel of suffering: God uses the suffering (which produces pain) in our lives so that we may be partakers of his nature. God's holiness and glory are closely related, and suffering is a means to both.

The writer of Hebrews continues in verse 11: "Now no chastening seems to be joyful for the present, but painful; nevertheless, afterward it yields the peaceable fruit of righteousness to those who have been trained by it."

Here again, we see the dynamic of a suffering (in the form of discipline) that is unpleasant and painful. Painful things are inherently associated by men with evil, negative, and joyless things. But in the hands of a good and potent God, suffering leads to joy. Godly discipline, which involves suffering, "yields the peaceable fruit of righteousness to those who have been trained by it" (v. 11). This peaceable fruit of righteousness is not some external, abstract substance known as "righteousness." Righteousness is the communicable character of God. The righteousness that is communicated to us is nothing less than Jesus himself, who is our righteousness.

Suffering leads us to Jesus Christ and, therefore, to glory and joy. Our suffering is used and meant by the Good Shepherd as his rod and staff which bring us comfort.[7] The rod is used to beat or hit the sheep, which is a painful event. But the result of the event is that the wandering sheep who will blindly lead themselves into pits, deserts, or predators return to their only safe place: the presence of the Good Shepherd.

How many times in the old covenant have we read of Israel, God's sheep, wandering (and not only in the wilderness of forty years)? Almost every page of the Old Testament records a wandering of God's sheep from him, only to be struck by the Shepherd so that the sheep may return to him.

How many times in our lives have we wandered from the Good Shepherd, believing that we may bless ourselves and lead ourselves to glory? And how many times has God used his rod or staff to strike us or drag us back by the neck to him? Suffering, in God's holy hands, is what gets our attention and wakes us from our nightmare of self. Suffering is what teaches or disciplines us to remember that it is he who has made us and delivered us, and not we ourselves.

We rejoice because our suffering means God is treating us as his children.

---

7. Comfort in this original sense means to strengthen, to give fortitude to someone, or to fortify them.

The Second Cup, Part III

Almighty God, Lord Jesus Christ, my great High Priest, who sits enthroned in glory in heaven: hear my prayers and supplications. I thank You that you willingly suffered for me and that You allow me the privilege of suffering for You, as well as for Your consolation that has helped me in my times of suffering and sorrow. Help me to look for ways in which I may suffer with others that I may more perfectly obey and please you. Direct my life and prayers today that I might learn obedience and faith. Give me a godly fear such as You had; be with me in my temptations and overcome them as You overcame the Tempter; teach me obedience in Your school of suffering, as You learned obedience; and grant me grace in my time of need, which is always now and in all things. Amen. (Charles Erlandson)

CHAPTER 6

Suffering Transforms Us into the Image of Christ

We rejoice because suffering transforms us into the image of Christ.

God, in his sanctified employment of suffering in our lives, is not only treating us as his children but is also using suffering to transform us into the image and glory of his only-begotten Son. Precisely because we have been united to the Son and are being transformed into the image of the Son, the Father treats us as the Son, including first his suffering but also his glory.

The process of being transformed into the likeness of the Son is a painful one and necessarily involves suffering. The paternal discipline of the Father is his constant process of training us to be conformed to the image of the Son. This persistent paternal pressure is something like the process an orthodontist uses to straighten out crooked teeth. Those of us who have undergone the penance of wearing braces on our teeth know how painful the process of tightening the braces is. But this pain is necessary in order to make that which is crooked straight.

God is the Divine Orthocardiologist: He's in the process of forming our hearts so that they have their correct, God-centered, shape.

This process of being conformed to the image of Christ is a painful one because it involves tearing down that which is broken and evil. It is painful because it involves cauterizing and surgically removing that which is diseased to allow something new to be made or grown. The old man in us does not die all at once but is painfully removed a little at a time, in the way that the Israelites conquered Canaan a little at a time so that the beasts of the field wouldn't be too much for them (Deut 7:22). We must mortify the flesh and put to death the old man in us every day, for if we do not, we find that they have grown back. This process is also related to the process of penitence, in which we not only confess and repent of our sins but also actively put on the New Man (Christ) by practicing his virtues.

We suffer, therefore, because this suffering is part of the process of purgation and sanctification, by which we are daily conformed to the likeness of Christ. God uses the evil of suffering in our lives as a means of making us good, that is, like his Son, in all things.

This process is also painful because we are loath to give ourselves up to God. We suffer when we willingly give up a part of ourselves, even though that part may be sinful, corrupt, and festering. Nevertheless, because it is truly a part of us, it is painful to give up. Anyone who has made a New Year's Resolution, a Lenten vow, or attempted to create a new habit knows how difficult and painful this process can be.

This process is painful and induces suffering because we are not metal but men. God does not act upon men as men act upon rock or metal. We are not inert material that he fashions in our bodies without also redeeming our minds and souls. We are not passive spectators in God's miracle of redemption and transformation. Instead, having been created in the image of God and redeemed in the image of his Son, we are made by God to be actual and active partakers of not only his grace but also his nature. Jesus doesn't want a lifeless mannequin for his bride but someone capable of loving him as he first loved us.

This painful process of being transformed into the image of Christ is glorious, for in God's using the evil of suffering to do good and make us good, the glory of God is revealed in us. Not only this, but both during this process and after, God shares his glory with us! For we must always remember that it was the cross of Christ that was his glory. We must also remember that the glory of the resurrection, therefore, also awaits us.

So then, we suffer because being molded and transformed into the image of Christ is a painful process. It is painful for us, as the children of God, to be corrected by him, just as it is painful for earthly children to be corrected by their earthly fathers. But the suffering of being made into the image of God is simply our spiritual growing pains, as we grow from glory to glory in the likeness of Christ. These pains are also the birth pains of the New Man, who is daily being delivered in our lives through a great and painful labor.

SUFFERING TRANSFORMS US INTO THE IMAGE OF CHRIST

Saint Paul teaches these things in Romans 8:

> For if you live according to the flesh you will die; but if by the Spirit you put to death the deeds of the body, you will live. For as many as are led by the Spirit of God, these are sons of God. For you did not receive the spirit of bondage again to fear, but you received the Spirit of adoption by whom we cry out, "Abba, Father." The Spirit Himself bears witness with our spirit that we are children of God, and if children, then heirs—heirs of God and joint heirs with Christ, if indeed we suffer with Him, that we may also be glorified together. (Rom 8:13–17)

THE GLORY AND IMAGE OF CHRIST

The many spiritual benefits that come through suffering with and for Jesus Christ may all be summed up by saying that *when we suffer as Christ, we receive the glory of Christ*. This glory that we receive is our partaking of the glory which is God's and which the Son shares with us through his divinized and glorified human nature.

The word "glory" is closely related to the word "image," for both words are visual manifestations of something powerful, radiant, and beautiful. When we behold something glorious, a sunrise or sunset, a beautiful woman, or children playing in complete harmony, our hearts leap, and we are led to rejoice and even to sing! "Glory" is sometimes employed in this sense of awe-inspiring beauty but is also sometimes used to mean the invisible made visible. Saint Paul explicitly brings together "image" and "glory" to make a theological point when he teaches that man "is the image and glory of God" (1 Cor 11:7).

The glory of God is, therefore, God's beauty and character made visible to and through the creation. It is the glory of God to be able to reveal himself through that which is not him, especially that which is so much less than him: his creation. The glory of God in the Bible takes the form of stunning physical phenomena, primarily visual in nature. In this way, image and glory are also related. Above all else, however, it is Jesus Christ, the Son of God made man, that reveals the glory of God. He does this not by his physical beauty but by his manifesting God's glory in his life of sacrificial self-giving and suffering.

Jesus, in his humanity, is the physical, visible glory and image of the invisible God (Col 1:15; Heb 1:3). He, as the Son of God, is also the firstborn of creation and his brethren. For this reason, the glory of God made manifest in Christ is frequently associated with his being not only the Son but also the firstborn (Rom 8:29; Col 1:15, 18; Heb 1:6). This glory is precisely what God shares with us through his Son, transforming us into the glorious children of God.

The *telos* or end of God's plan of salvation is that man might partake of both his image and glory. This is admirably expressed by Saint Paul when he writes:

> And we know that all things work together for good to those who love God, to those who are the called according to His purpose. For whom He foreknew, He also predestined to be conformed to the image of His Son, that He might be the firstborn among many brethren. Moreover, whom He predestined, these He also called; whom He called, these He also justified; and whom He justified, these He also glorified. (Rom 8:28–30)

God has called, elected, and predestined the church so that we might be conformed to the image of his Son and be glorified in him. The children of God receive the glory of God, even though they are his adopted children.

This same glorious plan is revealed in the book of Hebrews in the first two chapters. The Son, we read, is "the brightness of His glory and the express image of His person" (1:3). The Sonship of Christ is especially emphasized:

> For to which of the angels did He ever say:
> "You are My Son,
> Today I have begotten You"?
> And again:
> "I will be to Him a Father,
> And He shall be to Me a Son"?
> But when He again brings the firstborn into the world, He says:
> "Let all the angels of God worship Him" (1:5–6).

In his humanity, Jesus was glorified *because of what he suffered!* "But we see Jesus, who was made a little lower than the angels, for the suffering of death crowned with glory and honor, that He, by the grace of God, might taste death for everyone" (Heb 2:9).

Because Jesus gave up his life to suffer death for all mankind, the Father crowned him with glory and honor. But, as we've been saying, the Jesus who gave up all things, including his life, for us would not then turn around and hoard his glory or withhold it from us. "For it was fitting for Him, for whom

Suffering Transforms Us into the Image of Christ

are all things and by whom are all things, in bringing many sons to glory, to make the captain of their salvation perfect through sufferings" (Heb 2:10).

So, then, Jesus was glorified because of his suffering for us, and the way he brings us to glory is also through suffering.

This is why Christians suffer.

Although it's an inescapably difficult and painful process, "we all, with unveiled face, beholding as in a mirror the glory of the Lord, are being transformed into the same image from glory to glory, just as by the Spirit of the Lord" (2 Cor 3:18).

All of the other spiritual benefits that suffering produces in us are related to the glory we receive by being recreated in the image of the Son, who was glorified by his suffering and who glorifies us by our suffering with him.

Suffering with Christ, giving up ourselves for others through Christ, we partake of and are given the mind of Christ:

> Let this mind be in you which was also in Christ Jesus, who, being in the form of God, did not consider it robbery to be equal with God, but made Himself of no reputation, taking the form of a bondservant, and coming in the likeness of men. And being found in appearance as a man, He humbled Himself and became obedient to the point of death, even the death of the cross. Therefore God also has highly exalted Him and given Him the name which is above every name, that at the name of Jesus every knee should bow, of those in heaven, and of those on earth, and of those under the earth, and that every tongue should confess that Jesus Christ is Lord, to the glory of God the Father." (Phil 2:5–10; see also 1 Cor 2:16)

Having the mind of Christ, humbling and depriving oneself for the good of another, and, thereby, suffering for others, we are given the glory of Christ. Every act of self-giving is one more step in the process of growing from glory to glory in Christ, as we are made like him. By suffering with Christ, we give up love of self for the love of another. The more we practice this sacrifice of love, the more we are made like Christ, and the more the virtues of Christ grow and are strengthened in us.

We are now at the heart of the gospel of suffering, or how God uses our suffering to bring us glory.

Through Jesus, we rejoice in the hope of the glory of God (Rom 5:2), and Jesus in us is this hope of glory (Col 1:27). Not only this, Paul says: "but we also glory in tribulations, knowing that tribulation produces perseverance; and perseverance, character; and character, hope. Now hope does not disappoint, because the love of God has been poured out in our hearts by the Holy Spirit who was given to us" (Rom 5:3–5).

Notice how Paul expresses this truth: we *glory* in tribulations. By now, this should seem like an old familiar friend, so many times have we greeted this same truth in what we've been saying. Paul lists several spiritual benefits that come from godly suffering, but we receive all of these are blessings in union with Christ, as we put him on as the New Man.

> *Love divine, all loves excelling,*
> *Joy of heav'n to earth come down:*
> *fix in us thy humble dwelling,*
> *all thy faithful mercies crown:*
> *Jesus, thou art all compassion,*
> *pure, unbounded love thou art;*
> *visit us with thy salvation,*
> *enter ev'ry trembling heart.*
>
> *Breathe, O breathe thy loving Spirit*
> *into ev'ry troubled breast;*
> *let us all in thee inherit,*
> *let us find the promised rest:*
> *take away the love of sinning;*
> *Alpha and Omega be;*
> *End of faith, as its Beginning,*
> *set our hearts at liberty.*
>
> *Come, Almighty to deliver,*
> *let us all thy life receive;*
> *suddenly return, and never,*
> *nevermore thy temples leave.*
> *Thee we would be always blessing,*
> *serve thee as thy hosts above,*
> *pray and praise thee without ceasing,*
> *glory in thy perfect love.*
>
> *Finish, then, thy new creation;*
> *pure and spotless let us be:*
> *let us see thy great salvation*
> *perfectly restored in thee;*
> *changed from glory into glory,*
> *'til in heav'n we take our place,*
> *'til we cast our crowns before thee,*
> *lost in wonder, love, and praise.* (Charles Wesley)

CHAPTER 7

Suffering Unites Us to One Another

We rejoice because suffering unites us to one another.

One of the disguised blessings of ministering to those who are suffering is the way in which suffering binds us together. Rarely is this seen as powerfully as in war, which, although a form of hell, often reveals the glory of those made in the image of God. There is nothing like a good war to bind men together. Engaged in a battle for life and death, trained to act as one man, men form lifelong relationships and become a band of brothers in times of war. This sacred unity and brotherhood is sealed by blood and suffering, binding men together for the duration of their lives. All of this happens in spite of the evil nature of war.

Why should not the very real spiritual warfare in which Christians are all engaged so bind us together for a cause more just and glorious than any mortal war?

By our suffering, those who give and those who receive, those who suffer and those who minister to the suffering, become one in Christ as together they partake of the sufferings of Christ and fill up what is lacking in them.

The inner life of the Holy Trinity is an unfathomable mystery and yet one that has been revealed in part. Is it not possible that the binding together into one that occurs through suffering is a better picture of the life of the Trinity than picking shamrocks or contemplating the incredible edible egg? If God is love, self-giving love, must not this self-giving be at the center of the relationship between the persons of the Trinity? The Father gives himself up for the good of the Son and Spirit, the Son gives himself up for the good of the Father and Spirit, and the Spirit gives himself up for the good of the Father and Son.

As always, the way we see both the Father and the Spirit is through the Son. The most tangible revelation of the Trinity is the Father-Son relationship, in which the Son gives himself up to do the will of the Father. In some way, this seems to involve a giving up of a good that by right belongs to the Son. This giving up, therefore, is some kind of suffering. Speculative as the thought may be, a kind of suffering (sacrificial self-giving or love) may, in fact, be at the heart of the Holy Trinity, the Father, the Son, and the Holy Spirit.

THE COMMUNION OF SUFFERING SAINTS

Because we are united to God through Christ by our suffering with him, our suffering also unites us to one another in the communion of saints.

Man was made for communion with God. This is why all human history after Genesis 3 and before Christ is a tragedy. In "The Second Cup, Part II," we discussed our union with Christ, which is possible because of Christ's incarnation, and our baptism, which incorporates us into this divinized humanity of Christ. We also explored how this partaking of Christ involved not only a partaking of his life but also his suffering and death.

This profound mystery of union with Christ also yields the joyful fruit of union with one another. God made man one, but as a result of sin we fight, divorce, and hate one another. As a result of Babel, we are even further divided one from another as we drown the heavenly language of eucharist and doxology by singing songs of narcissism into the pools of our smartphones.

But suffering in and for Christ has the joyful consequence not only of uniting us to Christ but also of uniting us to one another in Christ. In the Apostles' Creed we profess "the communion of saints." This article of the Creed comes immediately after our profession of "the Holy Catholic Church." The two articles are intimately related, for the Holy Catholic Church *is* the communion of saints which we share.

Both of these articles, however, are subsumed under the third section of the Creed in which we profess: "I believe in the Holy Ghost." For the church has life breathed into her by the Holy Spirit, and the ongoing ministry of Christ in the life of the church is animated by the same Spirit. And yet even the Spirit is only the penultimate form or source of our communion:

the third section of the Creed is unthinkable without first having professed our belief in "God the Father Almighty" and in "Jesus Christ, His only Son, our Lord."

The communion we profess begins with God, the Father, the Son, and the Holy Spirit. God doesn't just *do* communion: He *is* communion, an eternal communion of three Persons. This is the basis for all other communion and the foundation for all reality. The communion God creates and seeks among his creatures, therefore, is an inexorable extension of who he is as the Holy Trinity.

The inner communion of the Holy Trinity is shared through the Son with his body and bride, and through this communion of saints, we share the divine fellowship together. We are brought into this communion with Christ by baptism, and it is perpetuated by partaking of the Holy Eucharist. This union is an ecclesiastical union: Christ is one with his one body and his one bride. It's not as if Jesus has more than two billion brides today or two billion temples, which then have to labor to imagine some kind of unity. Christian unity is only in Christ, which means in his body, the church.

This communion of saints in Christ manifests itself in many ways: unity in the church, unity in God, unity in faith, unity in baptism, unity in the Holy Communion, and unity in fellowship with one another (Eph 4:4–6). All of these unions are united in Christ.

In Christ, therefore, Christians across time and space have communion one with another.

But this communion comes at a price. This family reunion is a painful one, for reconciliation requires repentance and restitution. Reconciliation requires the pain of saying you're sorry for the evil you've done and the suffering you've caused. It requires repentance, in actually turning from that which within you is evil and causes others harm. It is, therefore, a profound act of self-emptying and self-humiliation which requires the giving of self and is, therefore, sacrificial.

In this way, reunion comes at the price of suffering.

But suffering is also one strand of the life of Christ that binds Christians together in him. Because Christ has transformed the meaning of suffering for the Christian and made it a means of union with him and, therefore, a means of bringing good, it is also a means of union with each other.

Saint Paul, again, has the most acute sense of the union among Christians that suffering brings. In 1 Corinthians 12, he teaches about the unity in diversity in the body of Christ that flows from the unity in diversity within the Holy Trinity. In speaking of the interconnectedness of the members of the body, he writes: "And if one member suffers, all the members suffer with it; or if one member is honored, all the members rejoice with it" (1 Cor 12:26). We all recognize this theological truth incarnated in our own bodies: those with migraine headaches or intense back pain know that the entire body experiences such pain, and not only the head or the back. Pain may even be referred or transferred from one member to another.

As Jesus lived out his life in Paul, Paul recognized what he first learned on the Damascus Road: that the suffering of individual members of the church is connected both to the church as Christ's body and to Christ himself. Christ's suffering, Paul's suffering, and the suffering of the churches *are all one*. When Paul suffers at the hands, for example, of brothers in the church at Corinth, he writes to the rest of the Corinthian Church: "But if anyone has caused grief, he has not grieved me, but all of you to some extent" (2 Cor 2:5). Paul writes to the church at Philippi, as well, that "Nevertheless you have done well that you shared in my distress" (Phil 4:14).

Conversely, the suffering of the churches entrusted to Paul's care results in Paul's suffering. Paul writes: "besides the other things, what comes upon me daily: my deep concern for all the churches. Who is weak, and I am not weak? Who is made to stumble, and I do not burn with indignation?" (2 Cor 11:28–29).

We've said that reconciliation comes at the price of suffering, but this is a suffering that is joyfully unitive. Paul writes in 2 Corinthians 7:

> For even if I made you sorry with my letter, I do not regret it; though I did regret it. For I perceive that the same epistle made you sorry, though only for a while. Now I rejoice, not that you were made sorry, but that your sorrow led to repentance. For you were made sorry in a godly manner, that you might suffer loss from us in nothing. For godly sorrow produces repentance *leading* to salvation. (vv. 8–11)

Here is another instance of the gospel of suffering: the sorrow of the Corinthians leads to their repentance and Paul's joy.

Paul's situation with the church at Corinth is God's situation with us and our situation with one another. We are divorced by our lack of love, which results in a painful separation. The one who has caused the pain by his sinfulness is grieved with godly sorrow over the suffering he has caused in one he loves. This sorrow leads first to a painful repentance and then to reconciliation. Paul says that this godly sorrow, which is a form of suffering, leads not only to joy in the one who was wronged but also to salvation for the penitent sinner.

SUFFERING BECAUSE OUR LOVED ONES SUFFER

Brothers and sisters: we need no further proof of how suffering is a manifestation of the communion of the saints than our own experience of suffering when ones we love suffer. Why should I care that someone who is not me suffers, unless, in some way, that person is a part of me, and I am a part of him?

When someone we love suffers, we become partakers of their suffering. Surely this is a sign, a symbol, and even a sacrament of how Christ continues to suffer with us in this life. Our suffering as a result of the suffering of others proves not only how united we are to one another but also how horrific suffering is. Our helplessness in the face of the suffering of others can be even more painful than the firsthand suffering we experience in ourselves. This secondhand suffering is merely one aspect of the collateral damage suffering causes. Suffering is, therefore, often compound in nature, encompassing not only the primary and most obvious suffering but also a cascade of secondary suffering in others. It is as if suffering is so powerful and immense that it spills out from the bodies and souls of the ones we love and rushes to enter us as well.

Suffering happens in community; suffering unites us. When our loved ones suffer, we cease to ask for whom the bell tolls: we know it tolls not only for our loved ones but also for us.

We often remain impotent in the face of the suffering of others. But we Christians know the One Person who is not helpless in the face of our suffering and who has chosen to do something about it. All that is left to us in such moments of helpless humiliation is to turn more fervently to the One who bears all of our crosses and who has taken all human suffering on himself. The additional suffering caused by the suffering of our loved ones is a particularly nasty species of suffering, but it is still one which Christ intends to use as a means of uniting us to himself.

Our suffering unites us to one another as Christians because it unites us to Christ and his sufferings.

> *The church is catholic, universal, so are all her actions; all that she does belongs to all. When she baptizes a child, that action concerns*

The Second Cup, Part III

me; for that child is thereby connected to that head which is my head too, and ingrafted into the body whereof I am a member. And when she buries a man, that action concerns me: all mankind is of one author and is one volume; when one man dies, one chapter is not torn out of the book, but translated into a better language; and every chapter must be so translated.

No man is an island entire of itself; every man is a piece of the continent, a part of the main. If a clod be washed away by the sea, Europe is the less, as well as if promontory were, as well as if a manor of thy friend's or of thine own were. Any man's death diminishes me, because I am involved in mankind; and therefore never send to know for whom the bell tolls; it tolls for thee.

(John Donne, Meditation XVII)

CHAPTER 8

We Suffer for the Good of Others

We rejoice because we suffer for the good of others.

Since we are indeed united to Jesus Christ and are his body, then we necessarily partake of his divine ministry of reconciliation and restoration. We rejoice, therefore, because we suffer for the sake of others. Becoming like the Master in all things, we suffer as Christians for the good of others, and this is a cause of great rejoicing!

Suffering binds us together in Christ because it gives us an opportunity to give of ourselves and to love the one in need, just as God gave himself to us. When we suffer for others, we rejoice because we are united to our Lord and Suffering Servant, united to each other, and experience the joy of giving ourselves for the good of others.

It is more blessed to give than to receive, and suffering or giving one's life for the good of another is the ultimate act of giving.

Occasionally, we suffer directly in the place of another, but this is relatively rare. We see this especially, once again, in the ministry of Saint Paul, who writes: "For we who live are always delivered to death for Jesus' sake, that the life of Jesus also may be manifested in our mortal flesh. So then death is working in us, but life in you" (2 Cor 4:11–12). The sentence of death under which Paul perpetually lived was God's means of giving life to the church. Paul adds: "For all things *are* for your sakes, that grace, having spread through the many, may cause thanksgiving to abound to the glory of God" (v. 15). Later, he also says: "I will very gladly spend and be spent for your souls" (2 Cor 12:15).

In his letter to the church in Philippi, Paul reveals an unusual moral dilemma: whether to live or to die. He chooses life, not for his own sake but out of his self-giving love for the Philippian Christians. Though it will cause him more suffering, Paul chooses life for the good of the Philippians:

> For to me, to live is Christ, and to die is gain. But if I live on in the flesh, this will mean fruit from my labor; yet what I shall choose I cannot tell. For I am hard-pressed between the two, having a desire to depart and be with Christ, which is far better. Nevertheless to remain in the flesh is more needful for you. And being confident of this, I know that I shall remain and continue with you all for your progress and joy of faith, that your rejoicing for me may be more abundant in Jesus Christ by my coming to you again. (Phil 1:21–26)

Paul sees his suffering for the Philippians in sacrificial terms, undoubtedly thinking of his participation in the self-giving sacrifice of his Lord. He writes: "Even if I am to be poured as a libation upon the sacrificial offering of your faith, I am glad and rejoice with you all" (Phil 2:17). Notice not only how Paul is willing to give his life for the life of the Philippians: he also *rejoices* in the opportunity to do so in the name of Jesus.

Although Paul partakes of the glory and joy in Christ in this life, the crown of glory in the life to come will be much greater. Paul's crown will be a glorious and heavy one: *the weight of the crown you will wear in heaven will be directly proportional to the weight of the cross you're willing to bear on earth.*

More frequently, we bear the suffering of others, not instead of them, but by offering consolation, comfort, and healing. In this way, we become partakers of their suffering and experience their suffering for their sake.

Charles Williams, the *other* Inkling, had a theory of suffering, which he called *coinherence*. Coinherence is akin to the theological concept of *perichoresis*, which describes the way in which the persons of the Trinity each interpenetrate and partake of the other. For Williams, men coinhere with one another. This is not a foreign doctrine to Christian theology, since we speak of being united to covenant heads: we are *in* Adam or *in* Christ. Williams saw coinherence as related it to the principle of substitution and the Christian mandate to bear one another's burdens.

Tim Keller sees this coinherence in terms of suffering, when he writes: "In the real world of relationships it is impossible to love people with a problem or a need without in some sense sharing or even changing places with them. All real life-changing love involves some form of this kind of exchange."[8]

Saint Paul expresses this *coinherence*, this suffering for the sake of others, in 2 Corinthians 4, when he writes:

> For we who live are always delivered to death for Jesus' sake, that the life of Jesus also may be manifested in our mortal flesh. *So then death is working in us, but life in you.* And since we have the same spirit of faith, according to what is written, "I believed and therefore I spoke," we also believe and therefore speak, knowing that He who raised up the Lord Jesus will also raise us up with Jesus, and will present us with you. *For all things are for your sakes*, that grace, having spread through the many, may cause thanksgiving to abound to the glory of God. (vv. 11–15, italics added)

SUFFERING EQUIPS US FOR CHRIST'S MINISTRY AND GIVES US A SHARE IN HIS MINISTRY

Even before we come to the point of sharing in and relieving the suffering of others, Jesus has begun the work of equipping us for his ministry by his transformation of our suffering. When we remember that our baptism is a baptism into the life and ministry of Jesus Christ, we will be prepared, like Jesus, to have the suffering in our lives be used for the good of others.

Our suffering prepares us to minister to others because it produces in us the fruit of divine sympathy: "sympathy" and "compassion" both mean "to suffer together." We call the sufferings of Christ on the cross his "passion," because on the cross he suffered with us and for us. This is the ultimate act and definition of sympathy or compassion. This sympathy is that which first belonged to God, who, in his mercy, sent his Son into the world to give himself for the life of the world. The writer of Hebrews says: "For we do not have a High Priest who cannot sympathize with our weaknesses, but was in all points tempted as we are, yet without sin" (Heb 4:15).

The sympathy or compassion of Jesus stains every page of the Gospels. Jesus famously wept for Lazarus when he died, even though he knew that he was going to raise him from the dead. Jesus wept over the city of Jerusalem in one of the most poignant scenes in the Gospels (Luke 19:41).

---

8. Keller, *Reason for God*, 201.

One of the ugliest of Greek words in form is one of the loveliest in meaning: *splagchnizomai*, which means "to have bowels of compassion."[9] Jesus's sympathy with humanity is not merely an intellectual idea but a love that is incarnated in the physical organs of his human body. Jesus has bowels of mercy on men five times in Matthew's Gospel:

1. when he looks and sees that the people are like sheep without a shepherd (9:36);
2. when he sees a great crowd who is hungry and needs healing, before he feeds the five thousand (14:14);
3. when he feeds the four thousand (15:32);
4. when he tells the parable of the unforgiving servant (18:27);
5. when he heals two blind men (20:34).[10]

When we are joined to Jesus by our baptism, faith, and suffering, his life becomes our life, and his compassion becomes our compassion. His perpetual sacrifice of himself to the Father, manifested in his perpetually serving others and giving himself to them for their good, becomes our sacrifice and oblation, which he now offers to the Father *through us*.

Jesus's suffering equipped him to minister to men, and so our suffering equips us to be ministers of Christ's life to others. Suffering unites us to Christ, humbles us, and enables us to sympathize with those who are suffering.

SUFFERING GIVES US AN OPPORTUNITY TO MINISTER TO OTHERS AND BEAR THEIR BURDENS

When we suffer, Jesus takes this opportunity to minister to us. What strikes us most about the ministry of Jesus in the Gospels is not all of the invisible ways he blesses the "rich" but the myriad ways He gives to those in need, the "poor in spirit." Once again, we're struck by how it is in the midst of suffering that God is most clearly revealed. For the temptation of the rich is to look at what is visible and think they've obtained it by their own strength and wisdom. But the poor know that they are in need.

---

9. The ancient Greeks saw the intestines as the seat of the emotion of pity.
10. Mark also uses the word when Jesus heals a leper in Mark 1:41.

We Suffer for the Good of Others

Having suffered and been ministered to by Jesus, we open our hearts to the suffering of others that we might do them good. The master in Christ's parable (Matt 18:21–35) has compassion on the servant who owed him an enormous debt. The servant, having been forgiven much and having been shown great compassion, should have learned compassion and forgiven the much smaller amount that was owed him. In the same way, Jesus's sympathy with us should create in us sympathy or mercy toward others.

Having Jesus bear the cross for us, we must be willing to bear one another's burdens. Having the cross, which we could not bear, borne for us, we must bear one another's crosses out of sympathy. In doing so, we must remember not just that this is a Christian obligation to love but also that in bearing the burdens of others we are only bearing a part of the one body of Christ, of which all Christians are members. We must also remember that the only reason we have riches and strength to give to others is that others have and continue to bear our burdens for us.

We are all called by Christ to be Simons of Cyrene, only we're not forced to carry a cross by the Romans: we've been *asked by the Master* to carry *his* cross. We bear the cross of Jesus in two ways: we patiently and joyfully bear the suffering he assigns us, and we bear the sufferings of others for his sake.

Even while we are responding to our own suffering, we humble ourselves and seek to serve others in their suffering. As we have been saying, the very fact that we, too, are suffering ought to make us more mindful of the needs of others.

As with Jesus, the suffering of others allows us to serve them in the Name and with the power and love of Jesus, who ministers through us. When we refuse to give to others in their need, we rob ourselves of an opportunity to see our Lord at work in our bodies. But when we look with bowels of compassion on the needs of others and do what we can to meet those needs, we discover what Jesus taught Saint Paul: it is more blessed to give than to receive (Acts 20:35).

This revelation of Christ to Paul is but one of the many inversions that take place under the miraculous ministry of Jesus. We instinctively believe that it is more blessed to receive than to give, and so we construct our lives to be receivers, something most manifest today in the consumer culture of the modern world. But God's kingdom works in a way contrary to the kingdoms of the earth.

The Second Cup, Part III

WE RECEIVE TO GIVE

We receive that we might give: we are served that we might serve. And when we give up ourselves in serving others, this is a form of voluntary and joyful suffering.

Giving to those who suffer draws us nearer to God because, in doing so, we are acting like those created in and restored to God's image. God is the giver of every good gift, but one of the primary ways he dispenses these gifts is through his people. Giving to those who suffer draws us nearer to God because, in doing so, we become like God.

To receive is human, but to give is divine.

One of the primary reasons we've been given the good things is so that we can give them to others. Although God desires for us to enjoy the kindly fruits of the earth, he also delights in us when we take his gifts and dispense them to others in his Name. We're all quick to forget that every good thing we possess, in reality, belongs to God. We are stewards of God's bounty, not only his material blessings but especially his mysteries (1 Cor 4:1). When we open our lives up to the suffering of others, we become instruments of God's grace and partakers of his self-giving nature.

Paul writes: "And let us not grow weary while doing good, for in due season we shall reap if we do not lose heart. Therefore, as we have opportunity, let us do good to all, especially to those who are of the household of faith" (Gal 6:9–10).

The diversity of good things we may give to those in need is as great as the manifold needs of those who suffer to any degree. When we imagine that the only suffering that matters is the suffering of persecution or suffering which is especially great in magnitude, then we rob ourselves of opportunities to minister in the name of Christ and, thus, bestow his blessing on others.

What we said earlier about how all suffering counts applies here. Every form of human suffering is suffering that God cares about and which He wishes to remedy through us.

If suffering is the lack of some good to which we have a reasonable right, then suffering is all around us, even if most of it seems small. But if God cares for the sparrows, does he not care about even our minor suffering? The suffering of children is often relatively small, for it is usually child-size. But children have many daily needs, which loving parents must meet. Suffering may be as sublime as being imprisoned or executed for Christ or as mundane and minuscule as a young child asking to have you tie his shoes. We might not consider untied shoes, unwiped noses and bottoms, unrelieved boredom, un-bandaged boo-boos, and the like as forms of suffering. But to little children, they are, and so we must enter into and heal such suffering.

Perhaps what keeps us from seeing such suffering as suffering is the joy of serving Christ's little ones and our own flesh and blood.[11] Sometimes the suffering is so slender and the joy so immense, that we fail to see the suffering. But other times the suffering is so gargantuan and our ability to help so impoverished that we cannot help but acknowledge the presence of suffering.

2 CORINTHIANS 1 AND THE MINISTRY OF CONSOLATION

Saint Paul frames his entire second letter to the church at Corinth in terms of Christ's ministry of suffering and consolation. After a brief greeting, his message corresponds closely with what we've been saying about the compassion of God and our partaking of this ministry of compassion.

> Blessed be the God and Father of our Lord Jesus Christ, the Father of mercies and God of all comfort, who comforts us in all our tribulation, that we may be able to comfort those who are in any trouble, with the comfort with which we ourselves are comforted by God. For as the sufferings of Christ abound in us, so our consolation also abounds through Christ. Now if we are afflicted, it is for your consolation and salvation, which is effective for enduring the same sufferings which we also suffer. Or if we are comforted, it is for your consolation and salvation. And our hope for you is steadfast, because we know that as you are partakers of the sufferings, so also you will partake of the consolation.
>
> For we do not want you to be ignorant, brethren, of our trouble which came to us in Asia: that we were burdened beyond measure, above strength, so that we despaired even of life. Yes, we had the sentence of death in ourselves, that we should not trust in ourselves but in God who raises the dead, who delivered us from so great a death, and does deliver us; in whom we trust that He

---

11. One of my greatest joys in life is being awakened in the middle of the night by a little child of mine who needs me. Though it costs me the suffering of lost sleep and the pain of rising and a stumbling, groggy wakefulness, it is pure bliss to serve such a little one entrusted to me and to whom I am an angel or messenger of God. So joyful is this peculiar service that I scarcely notice whatever suffering it costs me.

will still deliver us, you also helping together in prayer for us, that thanks may be given by many persons on our behalf for the gift granted to us through many. (2 Cor 1:3–11)

Paul's theology of the ministry of consolation (i.e., the gospel of suffering) begins with God. God comforts us in our suffering or tribulation, and for this, we must give him thanks and bless him, because it is more blessed to give than to receive. This tribulation is most acute in the sufferings of Paul himself, for he was tried to the point of death (vv. 8–10).

The blessing of God takes place in a specific way: by imitating God and partaking of his ministry of consolation. Though not the only reason, one of the chief reasons God comforts us in our suffering is "that we may be able to comfort those who are in any trouble, with the comfort with which we ourselves are comforted by God" (v. 4). Having received the mercy of God, we are merciful and do good to others, not just as a way of thanking God but also as a way of partaking of him and his glorious self-giving.

That we suffer in order to be able to help others who suffer is made clear in verse 5: "For as the sufferings of Christ abound in us, so our consolation also abounds through Christ." Our suffering in Christ brings us into union with Christ, and his life and suffering, and equips us to be able to minister as Christ to others who also suffer.

Verses 6–7 instruct us that our suffering is both for the good of others and also binds us together: "Now if we are afflicted, it is for your consolation and salvation, which is effective for enduring the same sufferings which we also suffer. Or if we are comforted, it is for *your* consolation and salvation" (italics added). Paul's suffering is for the consolation and even the salvation of the Christians in Corinth. Suffering and consolation exist to bind Christians together in Christ and, in some way, partake of his salvation for us. Paul goes so far as to say that the sufferings which the Corinthians Christians are suffering are the same as his.

The union which Christ effects through the suffering of his body is further expressed by Paul in verse 11: "you also helping together in prayer for us, that thanks may be given by many persons on our behalf for the gift granted to us through many." The shared suffering of God's people causes us to pray and give thanks to God.

We must never forget the necessary and unifying ministry of prayer. We may not always be able to help those who suffer. We may be too far removed in knowledge or geography; we may lack wisdom, strength, experience, or other necessary resources. But we can and should always pray, for prayer for others is a participation in their suffering. This prayer is an essential part of the ministry of consolation.

Prayer is an offering or sacrifice of self, for when praying for someone else you are spending your time and energy on him, and he becomes the object of your affection, rather than self. But because of the joy of serving others with Christ in this noblest of ways, we rejoice to give ourselves to another.

When prayer for those who suffer is answered, God gives us yet one more blessing and means by which we are united: together, as the body of Christ, we return thanks in the house of God. In Acts 12, after the martyrdom of Saint James, we read: "Peter was therefore kept in prison, but constant prayer was offered to God for him by the church" (Acts 12:5).

Peter suffered in prison, but while he was so suffering, the church prayed for him. We then read that Peter was miraculously delivered from prison, his chains fell off, and the prison doors opened of their own accord (all of which is a picture of salvation). When Peter came to the house of Mary, the mother of John Mark, he found the church praying for him. Through this, we see the participation of the church in Peter's suffering and are led to the conclusion that the prayer of the church had everything to do with Peter's deliverance.[12]

When God blesses us in our suffering, it is through Jesus Christ, who comforts and assists us through his Spirit in his church. Consolation, even if it comes through the life of one particular member, is a ministry of the entire church, and the gift of God is granted through many (2 Cor 11:1).

BY SUFFERING FOR THE SAINTS, WE ARE ANOINTING THE BODY OF CHRIST

Not only do we serve others *as Christ*: but we also serve others *as if they are Christ*. Who would not rejoice to serve his Master by serving those he loves and who are members of him?

Jesus reveals this to us in Matthew 25:

> Then the King will say to those on His right hand, 'Come, you blessed of My Father, inherit the kingdom prepared for you from the foundation of the world: for I was hungry and you gave Me

---

12. Paul experienced the same deliverance through prayer: "For I know that this will turn out for my deliverance through your prayer and the supply of the Spirit of Jesus Christ" (Phil 1:19).

food; I was thirsty and you gave Me drink; I was a stranger and you took Me in; I was naked and you clothed Me; I was sick and you visited Me; I was in prison and you came to Me.'

Then the righteous will answer Him, saying, 'Lord, when did we see You hungry and feed You, or thirsty and give You drink? When did we see You a stranger and take You in, or naked and clothe You? Or when did we see You sick, or in prison, and come to You?' And the King will answer and say to them, 'Assuredly, I say to you, inasmuch as you did it to one of the least of these My brethren, you did it to Me.'" (vv. 34–40)

Just as Saint Paul learned that to persecute the church is to persecute Jesus, so Jesus teaches that to minister to God's suffering children is to minister to the suffering Christ. There is a profound mystery here: it's as if Jesus is assuming that when a Christian suffers hunger or thirst, or experiences any form of suffering, it is Jesus himself who is suffering.

When we minister to any member of the body of Christ, we are anointing the body of Jesus Christ. What a joy and honor it was for Mary to anoint Jesus's feet in Matthew 26. If only we had the same opportunity!

Jesus says that we do, every day. We have the mystical body of Christ with us in the form of the saints (meaning all Christians), and we are to anoint it. Jesus has given you your spiritual gifts so that you might edify, anoint, and adorn his body (Eph 4:12).

What you do to and for your brothers and sisters in Christ is what you do to Jesus himself.[13] It might be the case that one of your brothers or sisters in Christ is among the poor, who are still with us, and that God is asking you to serve him in some way. It might be that you have the gift of teaching, and yet have buried that talent. Maybe your local church is looking for volunteers for an important ministry, and God is asking you to anoint his body in this way. Many of you will be called to anoint Christ's body with your tears in the difficult work of prayer.

WE HUMBLE OURSELVES THAT OTHERS MAY BE EXALTED

We rejoice when we humble ourselves, so that others may be exalted. This is the mind of Christ, revealed by Saint Paul in Philippians 2, who made

---

13. I make this point in my forthcoming book, *Love Me, Love My Wife: 10 Reasons Christians Must Join a Local Church*.

himself of no reputation but took the form of a servant or slave. Ultimately, this humiliation and self-emptying led to Jesus's exaltation, as it does for us. But Jesus's humbling himself is also the basis for *our* exaltation. Every time we give of ourselves for the good of another, we humble ourselves to exalt others.

Saint Paul's self-giving to the churches has a Christ-like imprint and character. To the church at Corinth he rhetorically asks: "Did I commit sin in humbling myself that you might be exalted, because I preached the gospel of God to you free of charge?" (2 Cor 11:7). Paul humbles himself in order to exalt the Corinthians.

There is, therefore, a mutual glory and exaltation between the one who suffers and the one who empties himself by giving to the sufferer. Saint James expresses it in words that are reminiscent of his greater brother: "Let the lowly brother glory in his exaltation, but the rich in his humiliation" (Jas 1:9). The brother who is poor in some good finds glory or exaltation in his poverty and suffering. But the rich brother finds glory and exaltation in his humiliation. This humiliation should take the form of giving from his God-given riches to the one who is poor in finances, health, spirit, or any other matter.

WE REJOICE BECAUSE WE SUFFER FOR THE GOOD OF THE WORLD AND THE ANGELS

It is not only for the sake of other Christians in the body that we suffer: if Jesus is living his redemptive life and ministry through us, we also suffer for the good of the world and the angels. When we suffer for and with Christ, we show forth Christ to the world for all to see. What an impression the early Christians made on their tormentors! How much some of them suffered, and how gladly they suffered it.

When innocent Christians suffer with grace and joy, they are imitating and partaking of the suffering of Christ in the way he suffered. Surely many Jews and Romans must have noticed that Jesus was innocent, and surely they noticed how gracefully, uncomplainingly, and even gladly Christ suffered at the hands of his tormentors. Surely, they heard him when he said, "Father, forgive them, for they know not what they do." Even a Roman centurion responded to Christ's sufferings with: "Truly this man was the Son of God!"

The song of the gospel of suffering was sung by the ascended Jesus to the first Christian martyr, Saint Stephen. When Stephen died, he died in union with his Master. Saint Luke records of Stephen: "But he, being full of the Holy Spirit, gazed into heaven and saw the glory of God, and Jesus standing at the right hand of God, and said, 'Look! I see the heavens opened and the Son of Man standing at the right hand of God!'" (Acts 7:55–56).

Stephen's suffering bore witness to Christ a second time: "And they stoned Stephen as he was calling on God and saying, 'Lord Jesus, receive my spirit.' Then he knelt down and cried out with a loud voice, 'Lord, do not charge them with this sin'" (vv. 59–60). What impression Stephen's suffering made on his witnesses may never be known.

That is, with one exception. For we read in Acts 7:58, "And the witnesses laid down their clothes at the feet of a young man named Saul." Jesus sang the song of the suffering servant, and Stephen faithfully heard it. Stephen sang it before Saul, and though it took Saul several years, he too heard it and taught it to many. How many must have witnessed Paul's sufferings and the way he rejoiced in them!

The song of the suffering servant is contagious.

When Paul and Silas were imprisoned, they were praying and singing hymns—*and the other prisoners were listening to them* (Acts 16:25). Why would Saint Luke record that detail? The implication is that the prisoners were hearing the gospel of suffering being sung to them. The fact that Paul and Silas could take pleasure in his infirmities (2 Cor 12:10) was a powerful sermon.

Interestingly, at the moment when Paul and Silas were singing in prison, there was an earthquake, as there was an earthquake when Jesus died. At Jesus's earthquake the Roman centurion cried: "truly this man is the Son of God!" At Paul's earthquake, the Philippian Roman jailer cried: "Sirs, what must I do to be saved?"

The sanctified suffering of the saints provokes spiritual earthquakes.

Polycarp was a disciple of Saint John and was martyred in AD 155. He learned the song of the suffering servant from Saint John, who learned it first from Jesus. The record of his martyrdom contains the record of how his suffering was for the good of others and made an impression upon even his tormentors:

> For nearly all the preceding events came to pass in order that to us the Lord might once again give an example of the martyrdom which resembles the Gospel story. For he waited that he might be

We Suffer for the Good of Others

> betrayed just as was the Lord to the end that we too may become imitators of Him regarding not only what concerns ourselves but also what concerns our neighbours. For it is the part of true and constant love that a man should wish not only himself but also all the brethren to be saved.[14]

A little later, the anonymous chronicler of Polycarp's martyrdom recounts how other Christians endured their persecution: "Some were so torn by the scourges that the structure of their flesh to the inner veins and arteries was exposed to view but they endured it so that even the bystanders were moved to pity and lamentation."[15]

Story after story, generation after generation, we discover this: the way Christians endure their persecutions is a powerful witness. A dramatic, more recent example of a persecuted Christian being instrumental in leading others to Christ occurred shortly after World War II. Japan's top pilot, Mitsuo Fuchida, was the leader of the Japanese raid on Pearl Harbor and the one who uttered the famous "Tora! Tora! Tora!"

Shortly after that, an American POW named Jacob DeShazer, who was a member of Doolittle's Raiders who bombed Tokyo in 1942, became a Christian while imprisoned. After being liberated, DeShazer wrote a tract about his testimony, titled "I Was a Prisoner of the Japanese," in which he spoke of his conversion to Christ and his forgiveness of the Japanese. Fuchida read DeShazer's tract in 1948, which led him to read the Bible for himself. Ultimately, he converted to Christ and became the leading evangelist in Japan.[16]

The reason we suffer is that our suffering shows forth the suffering of Christ for the world. We are the presence of Christ in the world today, by the indwelling of his Spirit, and in and through us, Jesus continues his redemptive ministry of suffering for the world. If the world does not see us suffer, and suffer with patience, faith, and even joy, then it may be denied the opportunity to see the suffering Jesus who came to save them.

This suffering of Christ is most visible in the Eucharist, where the bread is broken and then distributed. Christ's body is broken in the Eucharist, although not on the cross, so that it can be redistributed miraculously. Jesus's natural body had to die, resurrect, and ascend so that it could be miraculously transformed, multiplied, and distributed throughout the whole

---

14. Stevenson, *New Eusebius*, 23.
15. Stevenson, *New Eusebius*, 23.
16. Coffman, "Beyond Pearl Harbor"; "Mitsuo Fuchida."

church. This is the deeper meaning of the feeding of the five thousand: it's about the Eucharist, and, behind this, about the glorified natural body of Christ being distributed throughout the entire mystical body of Christ.

And so, as often as we partake and drink of the cup and eat the bread, we proclaim Christ's death, which we show to the world and even to the angels. The church, as the mystical body of Christ, is now, therefore, the suffering servant of God, and so in her body she suffers for the good of the world and to reveal Christ to the cosmos. The Eucharist is not only the sacrament of healing but also the sacrament of suffering.

We remember in the Eucharist not only the joyful and resurrected presence of Christ but also his death and suffering, which we carry about in the body (2 Cor 4:10). Jesus asks us to take this cup, not only that we might be blessed but also that we might become a blessing to the world. But to do this, we like Christ, we *as* Christ, must suffer with and for him, for the good of the world.

When we suffer for the good of the world, we must remember as well the angelic onlookers. Even the angels are instructed as God's love is revealed in the midst of God's suffering servant, the church. Paul speaks of the fellowship of the mystery of Christ, which he preaches "to the intent that now the manifold wisdom of God might be made known by the church to the principalities and powers in the heavenly places" (Eph 3:10). This fellowship of the mysteries of Christ, which enlightens even the angels, is, in part, the mystery of our partaking of Christ's suffering and resurrection.

We rejoice in our suffering because we are united to Jesus when we suffer for the good of others, bearing their burdens, offering consolation, and giving of ourselves and our substance.

> *Heavenly Father, whose blessed Son came not to be served but to serve: Bless all who, following in his steps, give themselves to the service of others; that with wisdom, patience, and courage, they may minister in his Name to the suffering, the friendless, and the needy; for the love of him who laid down his life for us, your Son our Savior Jesus Christ, who lives and reigns with you and the Holy Spirit, one God, for ever and ever. Amen.* ("Prayer for Social Service," 1979 *Book of Common Prayer*)

CHAPTER 9

Suffering Is an Angel and the World's Greatest Mnemonic Device

We rejoice because suffering is an angel and the world's greatest mnemonic device to us.

Although suffering remains suffering, in the hands of a merciful God, it is transformed into a species of angel. Suffering is an angel of the Lord because the word "angel" means "messenger," and God uses suffering to speak loudly to us. When God whispers in times of plenty, we are so busy pleasing ourselves that we often can't hear God. Suffering, however, is one of God's trumpets that blows loudly and arrests our attention.

And what is the annunciation of this angel of anguish? That God is very near and has entered into your suffering. Suffering proclaims that if we suffer *for* Jesus Christ, then we are suffering *with* Jesus Christ and *as* Jesus Christ. It trumpets the gospel of suffering in our lives.

Suffering is the angel of life announcing that Christ has come and that by this sign you shall know him. It proclaims the rightful King's judgment upon us: that we deserve this suffering and much more, but also that the price has been paid for this suffering, and that the King has come to make all things right. Suffering is the cross of Christ preached to us, to which alone is attached the promise of the resurrection.

We don't like suffering; we don't like pain. But pain is a messenger telling us that something's wrong with our bodies, mind, or souls and that we should seek healing of this pain. Pain is a messenger that often gets shot because we don't like its message. But ignoring the messenger or muffling him won't change the truth of the message or our underlying condition.

Suffering heralds the gospel: that man is broken and sick unto death and that God has sent his Son to heal (save) us.[17]

Suffering is not only an angel but also the world's greatest mnemonic device. We don't remember the way we used to, for now we have machines that can remember for us. The smartphone is not only the most powerful device man has ever devised but also the world's greatest distractor.

We erroneously believe that forgetting is not a sin but only a natural failing, such as not being able to dunk a basketball. In the Bible, on the other hand, forgetting God is not a minor peccadillo but the essence of sin.

The children of Israel were constantly judged by God because they had *forgotten* him. They got distracted by foreign gods and foreign wives and forgot the Lord their God. So God sent them the angel of suffering in the form of captivity. Hearing this trumpet blast, Israel awoke from her dream of self and returned to the Lord her God.

Too often, we're like children who are told by their parents to clean up their room and then immediately forget to. The sad fact is that the child never really treasured the parent's word enough to immediately do what was commanded. Usually, the child doesn't specifically choose to disobey: more commonly, he chooses to do something else instead of obeying. Getting caught up in the something else, he forgets to obey, for which he is fully accountable.

But God has an answer for us, for suffering is the world's greatest mnemonic device. For while we are prone to forget God when things are good, and hallucinate that we are gods, suffering evaporates our me-rages (mirages) and reminds us of who we are. Being deprived, poor, and needy reminds us better than anything else that we have been and forever will be dependent on God and his mercy.

When something hurts, it gets your attention. When something hurts, you tend to remember it. Like the hunger pangs during a fast, every pang of suffering in your life is God's reminder to remember him and turn to him. And, having turned to him, you are to place yourself in the loving embrace of your Father in heaven who promises to bless you in union with his beloved Son.

It is supremely counterintuitive to see God in suffering. But if, through prayer and perseverance, you practice the presence of God in your

---

17. In Greek, the verb *sozo* means both "to save" and "to heal."

Suffering Is an Angel and the World's Greatest Mnemonic Device

suffering, you will never be far from God. For suffering in this life is ubiquitous, the universal consequence of man's ruination of the cosmos. But this ubiquitous suffering is meant, *by God*, to remind you of his presence in and for your suffering.

Every time we suffer, no matter how small, we should be reminded of Christ's sufferings for us. Every time we suffer, no matter how small that suffering is, we should remember that we are partakers of the sufferings of our Lord and, therefore, partakers of his nature.

Perhaps the greatest problem of the modern and postmodern world is not secularism, atheism, or immorality but distraction. For a Christian who is distracted from God is a practical atheist for as long as he is distracted from God.

Nothing, not even the most provocative word in the sales world ("Free"), arrests the attention as much as suffering. As C. S. Lewis said: "Pain insists upon being attended to. God whispers to us in our pleasures, speaks in our consciences, but shouts in our pains. It is his megaphone to rouse a deaf world."[18]

This mnemonics of suffering, as we may call it, is embodied for us in the Eucharist or Lord's Supper. For Christ commanded us to partake of him in his supper by partaking of the bread and wine, *as a means of remembering him*.

"And he took bread, and when he had given thanks, he broke it and gave it to them, saying, 'This is my body, which is given for you. Do this in remembrance of me'" (Luke 22:19). We remember Jesus Christ every time we partake of him in the supper. But the Lord's Supper is not merely a way of mentally remembering Christ: it is the primary way he has chosen to be truly present with his people.

For *the best way to remember someone is to have that person present before you*!

Every Sunday is memorial day for the Christian.

The portion of the Eucharist where the congregation formally "remembers" Christ is called the *anamnesis*, which means "memorial" or "remembrance." We remember Christ by saying or hearing his words: "Do this in remembrance of me," by making the memorial Christ commanded.

In the traditional *Book of Common Prayer*, this memorial takes the form of these words:

---

18. Lewis, *Problem of Pain*, 91.

The Second Cup, Part III

> We, thy humble servants, do celebrate and make here before thy Divine Majesty, with these thy holy gifts, which we now offer unto thee, the memorial thy Son hath commanded us to make; having in remembrance his blessed passion and precious death, his mighty resurrection and glorious ascension; rendering unto thee most hearty thanks for the innumerable benefits procured unto us by the same.

This remembrance or memorial is a sacrifice of which we partake. Just as Jesus offered himself up for us, we join our sacrifice with his in the Eucharist and offer ourselves up to him.

The Lord's Supper is, therefore, no mere supper but a Holy Communion by which we are united to Jesus Christ and, therefore, blessed. It is a mnemonic device not by mental remembrance but by presence and participation.

The Holy Communion is a partaking of the sacrifice of Christ, including not only his death but also his suffering. Christ's body was broken and suffered for us, climaxing in the suffering of death. And when we drink the cup with Christ, it is not only the cup of blessing but also the terrible cup of suffering which Christ himself took for us.

But the Holy Communion cannot be a partaking of the suffering and death of Christ without also being a partaking of his resurrection. And so when we remember Jesus by partaking of him in the bread and the wine, we remember and partake of both his death and resurrection.

The word "eucharist" means "thanksgiving," and the Eucharist is the great thanksgiving for God's mighty salvation by the Suffering Servant who was raised from the dead. To give thanks to someone is to remember that someone. More than simply remembering that this person exists, and far more than merely going through the motions; in thanksgiving, we remember that someone has lovingly given something good to us. We remember the character of this person, and we are compelled to give thanks.

The Lord's Supper, which Christ has spread out before us, is called the Eucharist because it is the church's true Thanksgiving Day feast. And because God's gifts are so wonderful and blessed, we celebrate this truest of thanksgivings every Lord's day, and on other feast days in the church year. In the Eucharist, we remember God and the gifts he has given us, both heavenly and earthly, through Jesus Christ, who is our Daily Bread.

Suffering Is an Angel and the World's Greatest Mnemonic Device

Having remembered who Christ is, we remember who we are: baptized members of Christ's body, children of God, and inheritors of his blessed kingdom.

We rejoice because suffering is an angel and the world's greatest mnemonic device to us.

Suffering is a sign by which we remember and see that God is near to us and conquering sin, death, and the devil.

> *I came from far for thee,*
> *In love the long way down;*
> *I left My throne for thee.*
> *I wore a thorn-set crown.*
> *All this I did for thee!*
> *Wilt thou remember Me?*
>
> *I bore thy sins for thee.*
> *Wept tears of deepest woe:*
> *I bore God's wrath for thee*
> *To make thee white as snow.*
> *Could love do more for thee?*
> *Wilt thou remember Me?*
>
> *I tasted death for thee.*
> *Bore shame thy sins had wrought.*
> *My life laid down for thee*
> *To thee Life endless brought.*
> *What is My death to thee?*
> *Dost thou remember Me?*
>
> *I gave Myself for thee*
> *My all was freely given*
> *Thy Bread of Life to be.*
> *Thy Manna come from heaven.*
> *All this am I to thee.*
> *Eat and remember Me .*
>
> *I drank thy cup for thee.*
> *Thy cup of pain and tears.*
> *My hands have filled for thee*
> *My cup of sinless joy.*
> *Of blessing full and free.*
> *Drink and remember Me.* (Anonymous)

CHAPTER 10

You Can't Have a Resurrection without a Crucifixion

We rejoice in our sufferings because you can't have a resurrection without a cross or a cross without a resurrection. Throughout God's revelation of himself in the Scriptures, he never presents the cross of suffering without also giving the promise of the glory of the resurrection.

Fulton Sheen alludes to this theme throughout his magnificent *Life of Christ*. Most powerfully, he writes:

> If He was born of a humble maid in a stable, there were angels of heaven to announce His glory; if He lowered Himself to companionship with an ox and an ass in a manger, there was a shining star to lead Gentiles to Him as King; if He was hungry and tempted in the wilderness, there were angels to minister unto Him; if His blood poured forth in Gethsemane it was because His heavenly Father reached Him a cup.[19]

Sheen prefaces this by saying: "Hence, whenever there is suffering, death or even a humiliation mentioned, there is always the counterpoint of glory, victory or exaltation. Divinity shines forth whenever His human nature is humbled."[20]

No sooner had Peter made his great profession of Jesus to be the Christ than Jesus revealed the great mysteries of his death and resurrection.

19. Sheen, *Life of Christ*, 201.
20. Sheen, *Life of Christ*, 201.

Immediately after Peter's profession, "Jesus began to show to His disciples that He must go to Jerusalem, and suffer many things from the elders and chief priests and scribes, and be killed, and be raised the third day" (Matt 16:21). Jesus not only had to go to Jerusalem to suffer and die: He also had to be raised from the dead on the third day. You cannot separate Christ's crucifixion and his resurrection, and you cannot separate his humiliation from his glory. At the very moment Peter sees the glory of the Christ, Jesus begins to reveal his death and humiliation.

We've already explained[21] how the suffering of Jesus on the cross was also his glory, and how the resurrected Christ now eternally bears the wounds of his crucifixion. We should remember as well that "in the place where he was crucified there was a garden, and in the garden a new tomb in which no one had yet been laid" (John 19:41). Jesus only died as the seed in the garden so that he might be raised to new life, a life which he multiplies through his glorified and ascended body in his mystical body, the church.

Truly, at Golgotha, we witness life among death!

As heavy and painful as suffering may be in this life (and sometimes it is indescribably bad), Christians must seek the glory and joy of Christ in it. There can't be only a cross, not even in this earthly theater of suffering. For Jesus suffered that he might swallow suffering whole for us. Jesus died that he might pay the penalty for sin and, thus, conquer it. And he rose from the dead so that he could conquer death for us.

Since our suffering unites us to Christ, it necessarily unites us to the *resurrected* Christ (he's the only one there is!).

What if, like Saint Paul, the way we experience the resurrected Christ is precisely in our suffering? And what if implied in every ounce of our suffering united to Christ is a revelation of the glory of Christ in us? In this life, to experience the resurrected Christ is to partake of his suffering, and to experience the crucified Christ is to partake of his resurrection.

Behind every cross or crucifix we hang on our walls or necks stands the resurrected Jesus.

Christians would not have taken the cross as the supreme Christian symbol if the resurrection were not implied by and attached to it.

This is why the strange juxtaposition of suffering and glory is the essence of this book: it's the essence of how Almighty God has chosen to reveal himself in that which is small, weak, and which suffers.

---

21. See the Second Cup, Part I, chapter 4.

The Second Cup, Part III

Just as there is no cross without the resurrection, this life can't be a life of suffering only. We must believe in the hope of glory, the hope of the resurrection, and in a resurrected, ascended Lord who still comes to men in their suffering.

With every cross in this life comes the sign of hope and glory. Every time, for example, that a Christian dies, attached to the palpable pain and suffering is the fulfilled promise of God. For every time a Christian dies and enters into the presence of God, God's mighty victory over sin, death, and the devil is published both in heaven and on earth.

The cross and the resurrection *together* reveal God, not just one or the other. Therefore, suffering in our lives, and not only glory, is a revelation of God because it points to him and his work in Christ. The Almighty Ruler of heaven and earth is also the Suffering Servant. The God to whom all glory is due humbles himself for us. The resurrection is both the divine response to and the divine interpretation of the cross. It is the vindication or justification of Christ, the New Man, and the beginning of the fulfillment of God's promise not to destroy man but to restore him to life in God.

There are two related reasons why all of this is so counterintuitive. First, sometimes suffering, like the physical world, impresses itself upon us so heavily and clearly that we cannot see God or his glory in us. The glory and joy promised in our suffering are not what we see, unless we obtain eyes of faith. Without faith, we see a world that somehow created itself and somehow evolved a meaning and purpose. Without faith, suffering is just suffering and is the way of the world. It is an inscrutable, necessary, and inescapable evil.

But with faith in Christ, things always look differently. How God reveals himself is not how fallen men imagine him. Contrary to the common atheistic slogan, Christians have decidedly *not* made God in their image. Flannery O'Connor's "The Church of Jesus Christ without Jesus Christ" is much closer to what the world imagines and, therefore, sees.[22]

The second reason why what we have been saying is counterintuitive is that we know this life with its heavy suffering cannot be all that there is, and yet it appears to be. Men innately know that we were made for something better and that we catch glimpses of it in this life. C. S. Lewis has rightly said: "If I find in myself a desire which no experience in this world

---

22. See her novel *Wise Blood*.

can satisfy, the most probable explanation is that I was made for another world."[23]

Men instinctively believe in justice and fairness, that evil is evil, and that evil men must be punished. Men all hope that things will be made right, which presumes both that they are not and that for some reason they should be. And yet we do not see all things made right or all things put under Christ's feet—not yet.

This can only mean that the glory and joy in Christ which come from our suffering with him is, ultimately, an eschatological hope. The combination of suffering and joy point inescapably to a new heaven and earth in which all will be made right and all's well that ends well. Christ's death and resurrection, and our suffering and glory, are *sacraments* of God's promises to man. We both partake of the glory of the Lord and rejoice in him, and yet the fullness of this heavenly state still awaits us.

It's no accident that when we celebrate the Eucharist, we remember both Christ's death and his resurrection. The black and bloody background of the crucifixion only makes the glorious light of the resurrection that much brighter. By remembering Christ's death for us, we remember that there is a grave problem with the world and with our souls, but we also remember the God who is good and who is the solution to all the world's ills and suffering. By remembering Christ's resurrection for us, we anticipate the joys and glory of heaven to come, even while we bring our sufferings to the altar and join them to Christ's.

At the moment right before he raised Lazarus from the dead, Jesus said to the weeping Martha: "Did I not say to you that if you would believe you would see the glory of God?" (John 11:40). The glory of God is shown by the death and resurrection *together*. Lazarus's death and resurrection is a sign and sacrament of Jesus's death and resurrection.

Early in his gospel, Saint John records this about Jesus's disciples: "Therefore, when He had risen from the dead, His disciples remembered that He had said this to them; and they believed the Scripture and the word which Jesus had said" (John 2:22). John records something very similar at Jesus's triumphal entry: "His disciples did not understand these things at first; but when Jesus was glorified, then they remembered that these things were written about Him and that they had done these things to Him" (John 12:16).

---

23. Lewis, *Mere Christianity*, 135–36.

The Second Cup, Part III

Why the delayed recognition of Jesus? Because the cross only makes sense in light of the resurrection. But it *does* make sense, even in this life. For it was into this life that Jesus was born and in this life that he suffered and died for us. Human suffering only makes sense in light of the hope of the resurrection, both Christ's and ours in him. Therefore, the cross reveals the resurrection, and the resurrection illuminates the cross. Suffering promises glory, and glory justifies suffering.

We Christians rejoice because you can't have a resurrection without a cross or a cross without a resurrection.

The strife is o'er, the battle done;
The victory of life is won;
The song of triumph has begun:
Alleluia!

The pow'rs of death have done their worst;
But Christ their legions has dispersed;
Let shouts of holy joy outburst:
Alleluia!

The three sad days are quickly sped;
He rises glorious from the dead;
All glory to our risen Head:
Alleluia!

He closed the yawning gates of hell;
The bars from heav'n's high portals fell;
Let hymns of praise His triumphs tell:
Alleluia!

Lord, by the stripes which wounded You,
In us You've won the vict'ry too,
That we may live, and sing to You:
Alleluia! (Anonymous)

CHAPTER 11

Suffering is a Measure of God and Man

We rejoice in our suffering because suffering is the measure of both God and man. More specifically, suffering is the measure of our sin and what's wrong with the world, a measure of the goodness of God, and a measure of the glory and joy to come.

Suffering is a measure of what's wrong with the world. Pain, in general, is a symptom telling us that something's wrong. Judging by the amount of pain and suffering in the world, we should measure that something must be very wrong, indeed, with the world.

Man suffers, feels the lack of some good to which he has some right, because he's constantly dissatisfied with things as they are. It is not just our suffering in general but especially the suffering that comes from our dissatisfactions and disappointments that teaches us that something's wrong. And it's not just those who are poor or lack material things who are dissatisfied but also the rich, who despite possessing riches, fame, and power are not content.

It's never enough: we're never completely satisfied, and our dissatisfaction is a way to measure that there must be something more promised to us than this life.

What, then, shall we conclude about our suffering, dissatisfaction, and nostalgia? It seems logical to conclude *that man is haunted* and that suffering is a measure of the hauntedness of man. Man is haunted by his desire for what is perfect, for something that ought to exist but doesn't. Why are we so haunted? Because we were created for perfection, and yet by our sin, we fall far short of it.

Saint Paul reminds us of what we already know too well: "the whole creation groans and labors with birth pangs together until now" (Rom 8:22). We groan because there was once something better, and the promise remains that one day there will also be. We groan because we suffer.

Suffering is a measure of our sin.

This haunted dissatisfaction is a result of our sin. Sin is immeasurable, for the wages of sin is death, and man has yet to create a device capable of measuring the pain and destruction of death and all the lesser evils that have resulted from his sin. Each sin against God is a violation of his holy character; each sin is a divorce paper we have notarized; each sin is us signing our own death warrant.

But that's just one sin. Now imagine the sins of a given day, not just the obvious sins but also the ones we're too blind to see. Consider the sixth commandment and how it's not enough that I haven't murdered anyone today. Have I been angry with anyone? Have I wished anyone evil or withheld my forgiveness? Have I insulted or inflicted suffering on anyone in an unnecessary or malicious way? Have I withheld any good that I could have done anyone?

You get the idea.

Now multiply that by the sins of the estimated one hundred billion people who have ever lived so far. This is one way of measuring the magnitude of our sins.

Another way to measure the magnitude of sin is to consider the suffering in your life and those you know. That suffering is the result of man's sin, even when there is not a one-to-one correspondence between an individual's sin and his suffering. Your suffering is a measure of your sin and the sins of the whole world. But it is only a miniature of the suffering that is due to our sins, only a fraction of what we actually deserve.

As much as you reckon your suffering in this life to be, it is vastly smaller than the suffering that would be a just consequence of your sins.

The best measure of the size of sin is the suffering of Christ on the cross. The incarnate God, taking upon himself the sins of the whole world, along with their due punishment, is the truest measure of the magnitude of our sins.

Suffering is also a measure of God's goodness.

This is completely contrary to the common notion that suffering is a measure of God's nonexistence, apathy, or impotence. Romans 6:23 speaks of both the measure of sin and the measure of God's goodness: "For the wages of sin is death, but the gift of God is eternal life in Christ Jesus our Lord." The size of sin is that its just deserts are death. But the size of the goodness of God is Jesus Christ, the gift of God.

The magnitude of both man's sin and God's grace is Jesus Christ and his life of suffering. And when God meets sin, there is no comparison in strength or magnitude: Jesus Christ has triumphed over not only sin but also death and Satan.

When we suffer, therefore, we ought to experience and know not only our own pain but also the size of our sins and especially the magnitude of God's undeserved goodness towards us.

Suffering is a measure of the glory to come.

We rejoice because suffering is a measure of the glory that God has promised us. We've spoken at length about the glory and joy that is ours, even in this life. But this joy and glory are sadly and greatly attenuated in this life. Suffering, however, is a sign of the greater glory and joy to come, as well as a measure of it.

We might think of suffering as the dark part of the picture of life which highlights the part that is light and glory. In painting, the term *chiaroscuro* (Italian for "light-dark") is used to express contrasts between light and dark that the artist uses. Rembrandt, especially, was a master of *chiaroscuro*, but he only reflected a trace of the artistry and glory of God.

In Romans 8:18, Paul uses a kind of theological chiaroscuro: "For I consider that the sufferings of this present time are not worth comparing with the glory that is to be revealed to us." We can measure how great our glory will be by how much we suffer here. In reality, Paul says, there is no comparison. However great your sufferings are in this life, the glory in the life to come far outweighs it.

Do you want to know the true measure of the glory to come for those who love God? Then remember the time in this life when you hurt the most. However bad that is, heaven will be far more glorious than that experience of yours was painful.

We rejoice in our sufferings because they are the measure of both God and man.

> *O the deep, deep love of Jesus!*
> *Vast, unmeasured, boundless, free;*

The Second Cup, Part III

rolling as a mighty ocean
in its fullness over me.
Underneath me, all around me,
is the current of thy love;
leading onward, leading homeward,
to thy glorious rest above.

O the deep, deep love of Jesus!
Spread his praise from shore to shore;
how he loveth, ever loveth,
changeth never, nevermore;
how he watches o'er his loved ones,
died to call them all his own;
how for them he intercedeth,
watcheth o'er them from the throne.

O the deep, deep love of Jesus!
Love of ev'ry love the best:
'tis an ocean vast of blessing,
'tis a haven sweet of rest.
O the deep, deep love of Jesus!
'Tis a heav'n of heav'ns to me;
and it lifts me up to glory,
for it lifts me up to thee.
(S. Trevor Francis)

CHAPTER 12

Our Suffering Brings God Glory

At some point in our discussions of suffering and how they lead to our glory, a discomfiting thought occurs to us: haven't we left something—that is, *Someone*—out of the discussion of glory. While the focus of this work is the joy and glory Christians are promised in Christ when they suffer, our suffering is primarily for someone other than ourselves. More even than for the good of the world or the angels, we suffer for the glory *of God*.

Being the mystical body of Christ, being united to Christ in baptism and through suffering, we, *as Christ*, must glorify the Father in all things. This is the primary reason we suffer.

The gospel of suffering is that while God is glorified in our suffering, he then shares this glory with us. For being in Christ, we also have perfect reciprocity: God has so bound himself to man that he is glorified in us, as we are in him.

For this reason, we are frequently reminded to glorify God in all that we do. Every day, we pray the Lord's Prayer, with, in, and through Jesus, saying: "For Thine is the kingdom, and the power, and the glory, forever and ever. Amen."

Jesus commands us, in the Sermon on the Mount (of which the Lord's Prayer is a part): "Let your light so shine before men, that they may see your good works and glorify your Father in heaven" (Matt 5:16).

And Paul commands: "Therefore, whether you eat or drink, or whatever you do, do all to the glory of God" (1 Cor 10:31; see also 1 Cor 6:19–20; Eph 1:6, 12, 14).

Should not even our suffering bring glory to the Father, since Christ's suffering brought glory to the Father, and we are united to Christ as Christians?

The glory that we receive through suffering is, after all, the glory of God, which he shares with us as he gives himself to us through his Son. And although we are recipients of this glory, we are neither the first nor the most important recipients.

Christians suffer primarily for the glory of God. That is, God is glorified when we suffer with Christ as Christ suffered, for such suffering manifests the glory, the power, and the love of the God who has entered all human suffering to redeem it.

This is the teaching of Saint Peter, when he discusses the glory that results from our suffering. Peter reveals:

> Beloved, do not think it strange concerning the fiery trial which is to try you, as though some strange thing happened to you; but rejoice to the extent that you partake of Christ's sufferings, that when His glory is revealed, you may also be glad with exceeding joy. If you are reproached for the name of Christ, blessed are you, for the Spirit of glory and of God rests upon you. On their part He is blasphemed, but on your part He is glorified. (1 Pet 4:12–14)

In this passage, Peter has the glory of God foremost in his mind. We've spoken primarily of the glory we partake of even in this life, and yet we know that the fullness of this glory is God's already but only fully ours in the future. We rejoice even now, Peter teaches, but we will be glad with *exceeding* joy when Christ *in his glory* is fully revealed. And so our glory is experienced as a partaking of God's primary glory.

Even now, however, we are glad with exceeding joy in our suffering because we partake of the suffering of Christ, by which his glory is revealed. When the Magi stood in the presence of Jesus (and actually only the sign of his star), they rejoiced with exceedingly great joy (Matt 2:10). We can be sure that we stand in the presence of Christ in our suffering, Peter says, for it is only his presence that can bring us glory and joy.

Peter makes it clear as well that when we suffer for Christ, we must remember that it is primarily for the glory of God: "if anyone suffers as a Christian, let him not be ashamed, but let him glorify God in this matter" (1 Pet 4:16).

God is all-glorious and worthy of all glory! But what is this glory of God, and how is it manifested? The glory of the Lord is the beauty of the

Our Suffering Brings God Glory

Lord is the love of the Lord. The nature of glory is to be the visible, beautiful manifestation of an inner person. The glory of the Lord is especially the Son, who is the image and glory of the Father, *in his humanity*! Man, being made in the image of God and renewed in the image and likeness of the Son, has, therefore, a derivative or reflected glory.

> i am the moon, but YOU ARE the Sun,
> i only reflect Your eminence;
> all of the light that pours forth from me
> is but a fraction of Your brilliance.[24]

We humans can't actually *add* to God's glory: He has and always will be perfectly glorious. But we can *acknowledge* his glory; we can reflect his glory; and (joy of joys!) we can *partake* of his glory that he shares with us.

How is the glory of the invisible God manifested in the world so that we can see? Primarily in the Son, and yet the Son himself has gone into eclipse and prefers to reveal himself through the relative darkness of the moon. The glory of God was revealed in the self-emptying of the Son and the darkness on the cross.

God reveals his glory in us and in the world. It is easy to err by worshiping the creation (the error of primitive man) or by dismissing the creation as mere molecules in motion (the error of modern man). That is, we see God's creation either *as* God or as a sign of the absence of God.

In reality, *the whole of creation is a sacrament of God* and his presence in our lives. The sun and the moon; blue and red giants, white dwarves, neutron stars and black holes; apes and elephants; blue whales and giant squid; toads and nematodes; plankton and bacteria; redwood trees and sticker burrs; the bees and the ants; the earth, sky, and sea; the winter and the summer; the hot and the cold; ROYGBIV and the musical octave: all of creation is a sacrament of God's goodness and blessing.

But the glory of the Lord is seen especially in his Son. This means that one day we will see this glory as Saint John saw his glory: "One like the Son of Man, clothed with a garment down to the feet and girded about the chest with a golden band. His head and hair were white like wool, as white as snow, and His eyes like a flame of fire; His feet were like fine brass, as if refined in a furnace, and His voice as the sound of many waters" (Rev 1:13–15).

---

24. From an original poem of mine.

We should not be in too much a hurry to experience the glory of the Lord in this manner. When the disciple whom Jesus loved, who reclined on Jesus's breast at the Last Supper, saw this glory, he fell down as if dead!

The glory of the Lord is seen, in this life, not as the flame of fire but as the Crucified Son. We have spoken more than once about how Christ's glory, and that of the Father, is precisely his crucifixion for the sins of the world, along with his conquering of his enemies, accomplished as well by his resurrection.

The death of Jesus upon the cross glorifies both the Son and the Father. John's Gospel makes this point in four passages, of which we will consider only one.[25]

In his high priestly prayer immediately before his crucifixion, Jesus prayed:

> Father, the hour has come. Glorify Your Son, that Your Son also may glorify You, as You have given Him authority over all flesh, that He should give eternal life to as many as You have given Him. And this is eternal life, that they may know You, the only true God, and Jesus Christ whom You have sent. I have glorified You on the earth. I have finished the work which You have given Me to do. And now, O Father, glorify Me together with Yourself, with the glory which I had with You before the world was. (John 17:1–5)

We see here not only the glory that will come to both the Father and the Son through the death of Jesus but also that this glory, manifested visibly in the humanity of Christ, is, in fact, the divine glory which the Son has always had. These are not two glories, just as there are not two persons of Christ. This glorification of the Father and the Son is also a mutual glorification: the Father glorifies the Son, and the Son glorifies the Father.

But since Christ and his body are one, God is glorified in the suffering of his church. Saint Paul, a man of sorrows and acquainted with grief, reveals the mystery of God:

> that now the manifold wisdom of God might be made known by the church to the principalities and powers in the heavenly places, according to the eternal purpose which He accomplished in Christ Jesus our Lord, in whom we have boldness and access with confidence through faith in Him. Therefore I ask that you do not lose heart at my tribulations for you, which is your glory. (Eph 3:10–13)

---

25. John 12:27–28; 13:31–32; 17:1–5; and 21:17–19.

God's glory (his power and wisdom) are made known to the angels (powers and principalities) by the church. But the particular context for *how* God will be revealed or glorified is Paul's tribulations or sufferings. Furthermore, anticipating our next point, this glory of God revealed in his suffering body *also glorifies the church!*

Paul repeats this theme at the end of Ephesians 3: "to Him be glory in the church by Christ Jesus to all generations, forever and ever. Amen" (v. 21).

It is the glory of God to glorify himself in both his suffering Son and his suffering church. In reality, as we know, Christ and his body, Jesus and his bride, are one. While we might reflect on our own suffering and see nothing but shame and pain, God is glorified by the suffering of his saints. Jesus shares his glory with us, making us actual partakers of his glory and his mission to glorify the Father. Jesus has chosen both to reveal his glory and to glorify the Father *with and through us.*

Having affirmed the glory of God in our suffering, we return again to our own glory, derived, as always, from God. Hear Saint Peter once again:

> In this you greatly rejoice, though now for a little while, if need be, you have been grieved by various trials, that the genuineness of your faith, being much more precious than gold that perishes, though it is tested by fire, may be found to praise, honor, and glory at the revelation of Jesus Christ, whom having not seen you love. Though now you do not see Him, yet believing, you rejoice with joy inexpressible and full of glory, receiving the end of your faith— the salvation of your souls. (1 Pet 1:6–9)

Peter teaches that even in this life we greatly rejoice, even if this life is filled with trials and suffering (v. 6). Our faith, which is far more precious than gold and more valuable than we dare imagine, is being tested and even *glorified* by our suffering. The value of our faith is the value of Jesus himself, who has given us himself and claimed us for his own.

The value of our faith in Christ, *manifested* in our *suffering for him*, is Christ's eternal weight of glory, which he shares with us. We rejoice in our suffering, Peter says, with joy inexpressible and full of glory. There are those two words, "glory" and "joy," together again! (v. 8).

When God sees us, he sees his Son and his glory. We rejoice, therefore, because our suffering is transforming us into the likeness of Christ, who with joy inexpressible shares his joy and glory (the glory of the Father, the Son, and the Spirit) with us.

The Second Cup, Part III

We rejoice in our suffering because, with Christ, it brings glory to God.

> *Glory be to God on high,*
> *and peace, good will toward men.*
> *We praise thee, we bless thee,*
> *we worship thee,*
> *we glorify thee,*
> *we give thanks to thee for thy great glory.*
> *O Lord God, heavenly King,*
> *God the Father almighty.*
> *O Lord, the only begotten Son, Jesus Christ:*
> *O Lord God Lamb of God,*
> *Son of the Father,*
> *that takest away the sins of the world,*
> *have mercy upon us.*
> *Thou that takest away the sins of the world,*
> *have mercy upon us.*
> *Thou that takest away the sins of the world,*
> *receive our prayer.*
> *Thou that sittest at the right hand of God the Father,*
> *have mercy upon us.*
> *For thou only art holy;*
> *thou only art the Lord;*
> *thou only, O Christ, with the Holy Ghost,*
> *art the Most High,*
> *in the glory of God the Father. Amen. (The Gloria)*

THE THIRD CUP

Our Offering of Ourselves to God

CHAPTER 1

Introduction

The first time "take this cup" is said, the Lord speaks to us and offers us the cup his Son drank, the cup of wonder and the cup of woe. Seeing the woe, we say, "No! Take this cup from me: I will not drink it, for it's too painful, and I hope too little in what You promise."

The second time "take this cup" is said, the Father speaks to the Son, who drinks the cup for us. "Yes," the Son says, "I am willing to take this cup for the sins of the whole world. I offer Myself to You for the life of the world." The Son drinks the cup, becoming man, taking on all human suffering, and conquering sin, death, and Satan. In his suffering, the Son unites himself to his body, filling it by his Spirit with his own life.

It is time now to hear "take this cup" the third time. After Christ has taken the cup for us and united himself to us, we say, "I'll have what he's having. Father, I will now take the cup, but only with Your Son."

We take the cup, we pick up our crosses and suffering, and we begin to partake of the promised glory and joy which is found in Christ and comes through suffering. But, having drunk the cup with Christ and been transformed into his likeness, we, finally, offer the cup back to God. We also say: "Father, take this cup: I willingly offer it up to you. It is my life's blood—all my life and suffering. I freely, joyfully give it all to You."

By taking the cup with Christ, we become like God, transformed from glory to glory. Taking the cup which he offers us, only after he's taken it himself in his suffering and self-abasement, we offer ourselves to him in our suffering and self-abasement. Giving ourselves to God in love with the love with which he first loved us, we are bound together by the blood and by the cup.

We take the cup because our Lord lovingly offers it to us.

We take the cup because he first took the cup, in love, for us.

We take the cup because we know that by taking it with him, we are thereby united to him, who is the source of all glory and joy.

We take the cup for all of the reasons upon which we meditated in "The Second Cup, Part III."

But primarily, we take the cup because it brings glory to God.

If, as we have repeatedly demonstrated, the Father and Son are glorified by the Son's suffering and death, then we, too, will glorify God by our suffering with Christ.

For God takes the evil that men, the world, and Satan do, and he transforms it into his glory, which is the glory and joy of all who have communion with him.

> *Prayer: Our Father, who art in heaven, hallowed be thy Name,*
> *thy kingdom come,*
> *thy will be done, on earth as it is in heaven.*
> *Give us this day our daily bread.*
> *And forgive us our trespasses, as we forgive those who trespass against us.*
> *And lead us not into temptation,*
> *but deliver us from evil.*
> *For thine is the kingdom, and the power, and the glory,*
> *for ever and ever. Amen.*

CHAPTER 2

We Take This Cup, in the Garden, Praying the Lord's Prayer

Therefore, because it both glorifies and pleases the Lord (which must be the same thing), we take the cup when he offers it to us.

Having let go of self, and having abandoned doubt and fear, we take the cup.

But this is not a painless process. Let no one tell you that being a Christian is painless or easy. Dying to self, even a sinful self that was already sentenced to death anyway, is a painful process. Taking the cup comes at a price, and that price is Me: my self, my desires, my thoughts, my habits, my strength, my wisdom, my talents, my experience, and my riches.

Taking the cup is, in fact, a lifelong process, for it is life in Christ that we are offering, the same life into which we were baptized and the same life we receive each time we partake of his body and blood at the altar or table.

Jesus lived and grew for thirty-three years before he took the cup (in a way he had been sipping it slowly his whole life). Although Jesus had been practicing giving up himself to the Father and to men, although he had endured much suffering already, it was not easy for Jesus to take the final cup. He wrestled with his elected purpose, and he sought with anguish to be released from his terrible end.

We must, therefore, take the cup in perpetual union with Jesus, and this can only be done through prayer.

The Third Cup

Prayer is turning our hearts toward God, to converse with him in worship. It is the seeking of the kingdom, which is Christ, and through him the Father and the Spirit. It is the offering up of self to God, to rediscover him and please him. Prayer is the return to the union with God, for which we were made.

As George Herbert, the Anglican priest and poet, has said in his poem, "Prayer (I)":

> Prayer the church's banquet, angel's age,
> God's breath in man returning to his birth,
> The soul in paraphrase, heart in pilgrimage,
> The Christian plummet sounding heav'n and earth
> Engine against th' Almighty, sinner's tow'r,
> Reversed thunder, Christ-side-piercing spear,
> The six-days world transposing in an hour,
> A kind of tune, which all things hear and fear;
> Softness, and peace, and joy, and love, and bliss,
> Exalted manna, gladness of the best,
> Heaven in ordinary, man well drest,
> The milky way, the bird of Paradise,
> Church-bells beyond the stars heard, the soul's blood,
> The land of spices; something understood.

Prayer is always through Christ, our High Priest, by the ministry of the Spirit. Our prayer is always united to his prayer, just as our lives are united to his. Prayer is, therefore, a suitable companion for our suffering, since both are means by which Jesus unites himself to us.

To pray is to take the cup with Jesus Christ.

To pray is to offer yourself to God as a living sacrifice, to empty yourself of all but God and to exchange your will for his will. After we have drained the cup ourselves, both in suffering and in prayer, God refills the cup with his Son.

To pray is to seek heaven, which is God, Who is the focus of all prayer. Let us now meditate on the Lord's Prayer as a means of taking the cup. Let us take the cup with Jesus in the garden of Gethsemane as we, like and with him, wrestle with the agony of our suffering and giving self back to God.

PRAYING THE LORD'S PRAYER WITH CHRIST IN THE GARDEN

We should imagine that Jesus was praying the Lord's Prayer, or something very like it, both when in the garden and when on the cross.

Suppose you knelt before a crucifix or cross and prayed the Lord's Prayer with the Lord's suffering in mind. Imagine his agony in the garden, as he wrestled with the terrible cup in his hand. To drink or not to drink? Imagine that Jesus has said "Yes," and is now on the cross, praying to the Father as he bears your suffering and sins.

Behold the love of God poured out on man by the sacrificial obedience of him who is the Bread of Life. Behold the Lamb of God who takes away the sins of the world, rebukes all temptation and tempters, and undoes the evil of both devil and man.

Let us pray the Lord's Prayer in the garden of Gethsemane with Jesus, saying:

Our Father—Remember that your Lord prayed passionately to the Father in the garden, and he is now interceding before the Father for you. He came to do the will of the Father, whose will was that the Son and all in union with him take the cup. Remember the words of the God on the cross, who said, "Whoever has seen me has seen the Father" (John 14:9).

Imagine that, by offering yourself and suffering with the Son, you, too, may now call God "Father."

Who art in heaven—Heaven always meets earth on the mountain. Who may ascend the hill of the Lord, that terrible hill, Golgotha, where heaven and earth met in the person of Jesus Christ, joined by the Father and the Spirit? Only the Son, both God and man, for only he has clean hands and a pure heart.

Heaven has lighted on the cross, for God was surely there in the person of the Son. Heaven and earth have met in Christ, who is not only King of heaven and earth but also its Suffering Servant.

God is in our suffering; *heaven is in our hurts.*

On the cross, heaven was opened for all believers because Jesus is heaven. Today, he says to all who believe but suffer, "you shall be with Me in Paradise." The heavenly angels that once guarded the garden and barred man from re-entrance now usher us into heaven and paradise at the tomb of Jesus.

Hallowed be Thy Name—Here is that name exalted above every name. Look up, there it is, nailed to a cross, and exalted by suffering. I have glorified Your name and will glorify it in my mystical body as it suffers.

The Third Cup

Thy kingdom come—If you want to be great in the kingdom of heaven, learn to be the servant of all. The King is brought to his knees, pleading for his life, to be delivered from sinful men. But his glory is in suffering and dying for his false witnesses, unjust judges, and guilty executioners. In solidarity with man, he prays for the kingdom to be removed, for the cup is the royal chalice, and he is not only the King's wine taster and cupbearer but also the King himself. But he knows he will only be King if he bears the cup, for this is his glory and the glory of the Father. It is the way he rules and establishes his kingdom.

Here is the King and, therefore, the kingdom, suffering on the cross.

If you want to be great in the kingdom of heaven, in Christ, you, too, must take the cup! For it is by suffering and by his cross, along with his resurrection, that Jesus defeats the powers of evil and establishes his kingdom.

Thy will be done—This is the essential prayer of Jesus and all who are in him: that the will of the Father would be done. All else hangs on this. Are we willing to take up our crosses, deny ourselves, and follow Jesus in doing the will of the Father?

To make this choice, to take this cup, requires suffering and dying to self. To reject it is to recapitulate the fall—to see Jesus get off his knees in Gethsemane and retire somewhere in Galilee. To reject the cup is to have a Jesus without a cross, which means a Jesus with neither obedience nor resurrection.

When I gaze intently at the cross, looking at Jesus on my knees, I see myself looking at myself. For I must take up my cross today and obey; for this is how heaven has come to earth, through the obedience that led to the cross.

If I love Jesus and would be united with him, and if I would seek his glory and that of the Father: then I must take the cup of suffering that the Father has offered to me. But I will only take it because Jesus promises to take it with me.

Yes, Lord, I will take the cup.

Yes, Lord, with Your Son I am able to take the cup.

On earth, as it is in heaven—As the Son fulfilled the will of the Father by coming down from heaven to earth, he also fulfilled the will of the Father while on earth. Now that his glorified humanity is in heaven, he has sent the Spirit to help us pray here on earth. Every moment Jesus obeyed, he turned earth into heaven, the place of God's presence and blessing, the place of perfect peace, and the place of perfect love and obedience.

We Take This Cup, in the Garden, Praying the Lord's Prayer

Although the garden of Gethsemane and Golgotha looked and felt like hell, Jesus transformed them into heaven. For God, as we have been saying, transforms evil into good, and he is transforming us from the children of the earth to the children of heaven.

The coming of God's kingdom, in the Lord's Prayer and in our lives, is, therefore, organically connected to the will of the Father being done. If we want to see God, if we want to enter heaven, then we must obediently take the cup.

Give us this day our daily bread—Jesus prayed in the garden for his daily bread: the Father gave him the cup to drink.

Jesus refused the wine changed to vinegar on the cross: the Father gave him his daily bread to sustain him on the cross. For what was the daily bread to Christ, who is our daily bread, but to do the will of the Father (John 4:34).

Jesus *is* our Daily Bread, and he offers himself in every moment of every day. Our daily bread each day is the day itself and all that God has ordained in it for us, because God offers his Son to us in every grain of every day, including the bread of sorrow and suffering.

When the Father sent the angel to Jesus in the garden, the angel didn't come to change the will of the Father. The angel didn't come to "answer" Jesus's prayer and give him what he had asked for, to be released from his terrible ministry and mission. That angel was, in fact, Jesus's daily bread to enable him to bring in the kingdom of heaven by obeying the will of the Father in saving the world.

Pray with Jesus for divine strength to do the difficult thing that the Father has asked you to do. *Only if you first eat your Daily Bread, which is Jesus Christ, will you be able to take the cup of obedience and suffering he also offers.*

And forgive us our trespasses, as we forgive those who trespass against us—Though Jesus himself did not commit any trespasses, he was about to take all our sins upon himself and bear our pain, death, and penalty. In taking the cup for us, Jesus forgave us all our sins.

On the cross, with arms outstretched to encompass the whole world, suspended between heaven and earth, God forgave the sins of the world. Jesus took the cup. At that very moment, the kingdom was coming in even greater power and glory.

As we hang on the cross and suffer with Jesus, as we take the terrible cup with him, we are forgiven in him and are given the God-like power to forgive others.

And lead us not into temptation, but deliver us from evil—Jesus was tempted to take the easy way out; in fact, he prayed three times for the Father to take the cup from him. Jesus, the Second Adam, was being tempted here in the garden, just as Adam and Eve were tempted in the garden. And yet he was ever without sin. He, at that moment, was delivering us from evil and the Evil One, from suffering and Sin, and from death. His kingdom was coming victoriously through his divine victimhood.

At the cross, Jesus took all the evil of the world and transformed it into good. God took the worst thing man could ever do and made it into the best thing that he ever did.

This is the meaning of Christian suffering.

For Thine is the kingdom, and the power, and the glory, for ever and ever, Amen.—When Jesus wrestled with himself and the devil over the taking of the cup, Jesus chose to take it for you and for me. He did it to glorify the Father, first and foremost, but he also did it so that we might enter the kingdom of heaven, praise God's mighty power, and enjoy and glorify him forever. Jesus did not seek his own glory, but since he glorified the Father, he himself, in his humanity, was also glorified.

And if we will but take the cup with him, seeking first the glory of God and his kingdom, his Son, he promises to add to us joy and glory, too.

Do not take the cup of suffering without sacrificing yourself to God in prayer.

> *Prayer: Our Father*
> *who art in heaven*
> *hallowed be thy Name*
> *thy kingdom come*
> *thy will be done*
> *on earth as it is in heaven.*
> *Give us this day our daily bread.*
> *And forgive us our trespasses,*
> *as we forgive those who trespass against us.*
> *And lead us not into temptation,*
> *but deliver us from evil.*
> *For thine is the kingdom, and the power, and the glory,*
> *for ever and ever. Amen.*

CHAPTER 3

God Is Redeeming Man by Man

Great is the mystery of suffering, and great is the mystery of Christ in us and we in him!

Christ, as we have said, continues to offer up himself to the Father as a sacrificial offering of obedience in suffering—through us! *This is why we suffer.* We each offer up ourselves as living sacrifices of Christ, crucifying the old man in us through Jesus Christ.

We are united to Jesus Christ in his suffering, as he is united to us in ours. God is, therefore, redeeming man by man: the Second Adam recapitulates the first Adam and lives the life man was supposed to live. God assumed human nature that he might redeem human nature through the perfect human nature that is now forever joined to the divine nature.

God made someone worthy of being his bride: the church. She must, therefore, be glorious enough to be married to and made one with Christ. When Adam surveyed the creatures God had made, none was fit to be his wife, until Eve. Jesus has, likewise, made a bride fit to become one flesh with him, and that bride is the church.

Redeemed by and united to Christ, we have a part to play with him in his redemption of the world.

No one but you can offer yourself up to the Father through the Son.

Each of you has a noble and unique part to play in Jesus's redemption of the world. Through you, he is redeeming your suffering, your life, and the suffering and lives of others.

This is the meaning of human suffering.

What a high calling God has in mind for us!

Therefore, we are not only worthy of being redeemed but also, as Christ's body, are participants *in* Christ's redemption. He is redeeming us through us, as his divine body of grace.

The mysterious miracle of what we have been trying to say, especially about filling up what is lacking in Christ's sufferings, did not escape the attention of Pope John Paul II, who wrote that the church

> completes that suffering *just as the Church completes the redemptive work of Christ.* The mystery of the Church—that body which completes in itself also Christ's crucified and risen body—indicates at the same time the space or context in which human sufferings complete the sufferings of Christ. Only within the radius and dimension of the Church as the Body of Christ, which continually develops in space and time, can one think and speak of 'what is lacking' in the sufferings of Christ.[26]

As it turns out, the mystery of God's eternal love within himself as the Father, the Son, and the Spirit, has been poured out into man—in his creation, in the incarnation, and in the continuing redemption of the world through the Son in his body, the church.

In some way beyond human imagining and expression, God's eternal self-giving love looks like the Son hanging on the cross, applied to fallen man, who stands under the condemnation of God. And, being truly united to the Son, the church is the image of this same Christ who hung on the accursed tree.

It turns out that God's eternal love is at the heart of all human suffering. One who unites his suffering to that of Christ with faith

> *is serving,* like Christ, *the salvation of his brothers and sisters.* Therefore, he is carrying out an irreplaceable service. In the Body of Christ, which is ceaselessly born of the cross of the Redeemer, it is precisely suffering permeated by the spirit of Christ's sacrifice that is *the irreplaceable mediator and author of the good things* which are indispensable to the world's salvation.[27]

Filling up what is lacking is another way of saying that God has become man and so united himself to man in Christ that redeemed man, the body of Christ, now participates directly in the redemption of the world.

---

26. John Paul II, *Christian Meaning of Human Suffering*, 61. Italics in the original.
27. John Paul II, *Christian Meaning of Human Suffering*, 77.

God Is Redeeming Man by Man

Suffering, therefore, leads to glory in this astounding way: that the glory of man is now to share in the redemptive work of God by his suffering.

The glory of God is to empty himself and share himself with man, even in the glorious work of redemption, which is purely God's. The glory of man, a lesser but participatory glory, is to receive this gift of the life and work of Jesus and give it back to God by partaking of redemption through suffering.

Only by first taking the cup with Christ, can we then give the cup of suffering and life back to God.

Shall not we your sorrow share
And from worldly joys abstain,
Fasting with unceasing prayer,
Strong with you to suffer pain?

Then, if Satan on us press,
Flesh or spirit to assail,
Victor in the wilderness,
Grant we may not faint nor fail!

So shall we have peace divine;
Holier gladness ours shall be.
Round us, too, shall angels shine,
Such as served You faithfully.

Keep, O keep us, Savior dear,
Ever constant by your side,
That with you we may appear
At th'eternal Eastertide.
(George Hunt Smyttan)

CHAPTER 4

We Offer Our Cup of Suffering to the Father

TAKING THE CUP

We have come to a crux of this book.
Will you take the cup?
Knowing that our good God transforms evil into good and has sent his Son into the world to redeem suffering:
Comprehending that the Son took the cup and suffered and died for you and now offers union with him:
Accepting the grace of the Spirit in your hearts, which rejoice in the glory which is Christ's and which he shares with you:
Will you take the cup?
The question isn't whether or not you will suffer: to be human is to suffer.
The question isn't whether to accept your suffering or not: stoics accept their suffering.
The question is whether you will lift the cup to your lips, knowing that your suffering is an evil contrary to the goodness of God but also knowing that God intends to use it to bring you glory and joy.
The question is Jesus's question to Peter after the resurrection: "Do you love Me?"

We Offer Our Cup of Suffering to the Father

The Holy Scriptures are clear: God intends to use suffering in the life of believers to bring them glory and honor through the Son. As the Scriptures teach: "rejoice to the extent that you partake of Christ's sufferings, that when His glory is revealed, you may also be glad with exceeding joy" (1 Pet 4:13).

The Holy Word himself is clear by the voice of his actions: "For it was fitting for Him, for whom are all things and by whom are all things, in bringing many sons to glory, to make the captain of their salvation perfect through sufferings" (Heb 2:10).

The Holy Spirit, whispering in your heart, is clear: "I want Jesus and know that to have him, I must take the cup with him and *for* him."

Without Christ, we will not take the cup. Even those who truly love Jesus will often refuse the cup of suffering and not receive it with faith.

But with Christ, we gladly take the cup for the joy and glory set before us. This is not just the eternal, immeasurable glory and joy of the life to come but also the joy and glory that Christ sets before us even now because he is *in* the cup. The suffering remains evil, but God transforms its significance and effect into a cup of blessing.

The cup which Jesus is asking us to take is the cup that was promised us at our baptism, when we were baptized into and united with the death and resurrection of Jesus Christ. It is the cup of the crucified Jesus as well as the cup of the resurrected Jesus because you can't have a crucifixion without a resurrection nor a resurrection without a crucifixion.

To take the cup is to say Mary's "yes" to God when she, too, was promised something too wonderful for words and almost too wonderful for belief.

To take the cup is to pray with Mary's Son in the garden, when he was wrestling with the cup: "nevertheless not My will, but Yours, be done." It is to partake of God's "yes" to all he has ever said or promised. And this "yes" is Christ: "for all the promises of God in Him are Yes, and in Him Amen, to the glory of God through us" (1 Cor 1:20).

To take the cup is to pray with Jesus: "Thy kingdom come, Thy will be done, on earth as it is in heaven. Give us this day our Daily Bread." It is to pray this, knowing that *Jesus is the Daily Bread by whom we take the daily cup.*

To take the cup is to partake of the Tree of Life and undo Adam's "no" and curse. To take the cup is to be escorted by angels into the new and better garden, and to be today in paradise with Jesus, although we are but thieves, hanging on the cross for our own sins and crimes.

Are you able to be baptized with the baptism with which he was baptized?

No, but if you have been baptized, you have *already* been baptized into Christ and his life and death.

Are you able to take this cup? Not by yourself.

But remember that the whole point of taking the cup is to partake of Jesus, who has already taken the cup for you.

Take the cup.

> For I received from the Lord that which I also delivered to you: that the Lord Jesus on the same night in which He was betrayed took bread; and when He had given thanks, He broke it and said, "Take, eat; this is My body which is broken for you; do this in remembrance of Me." In the same manner He also took the cup after supper, saying, "This cup is the new covenant in My blood. This do, as often as you drink it, in remembrance of Me." For as often as you eat this bread and drink this cup, you proclaim the Lord's death till He comes. (1 Cor 11:23–26)

TAKING THE CUP AND OFFERING IT TO THE LORD

After having received the cup from the Lord, and after having taken it, we are filled with Christ and his afflictions but also with Christ and his glory. These things fill us with joy, if we are alive to the Lord! After having received the cup and drunk it with Christ, being filled with Christ, we are now able to offer it back to the Father in Christ. It is now not only Christ's suffering and sacrifice that glorify the Father and redeem the world but also ours, in Christ.

Lifting the cup to your lips and drinking (miracle of miracles!) is the same as offering up yourself to the Lord. To say "not my will but Thy will" is to receive not a cup of woe but the cup of blessing. It is to reopen paradise for business. It is, truly, to partake of Christ and his "full, perfect, and sufficient sacrifice, oblation, and satisfaction, for the sins of the whole world."[28]

Our suffering, though it might be imposed from the outside, and though it is an evil in and of itself, is something we should willingly offer up to the Lord as a sacrifice of thanksgiving and praise. For just as God uses the bread and the wine to give us the body and blood of his Son, so he uses our suffering to give us his Son.

---

28 Traditional *Book of Common Prayer* "Prayer of Consecration."

Jesus took the cup of all human suffering, deprivation, and hurt and offered it to the Father. At the same time, he offered his life to the Father as the sacrifice for the sins of the world.

What could we possibly offer to God in response to his transcendent mercies? Whatever it is, we know it would be too small to compare with his great gifts.

But we know the answer to this question, for God himself has told us what pleases him. And what pleases him immeasurably is for us to give ourselves, including our suffering, back to him. This oblation, or offering, of self is itself a source of suffering, since we are addicted to ourselves and only painfully relinquish trust in ourselves.

There is not any part of me that doesn't belong to God and which I should not offer back to him. When humble Isaac went up to Mount Moriah with Abraham to sacrifice, he innocently asked, "Look, the fire and the wood, but where is the lamb for a burnt offering?" (Gen 22:7).

We might look as puzzled when God asks us to sacrifice to him. But, having heard the gospel of suffering, we have the epiphany that *we* are the sacrifice and always have been. God was never as interested in the blood of bulls and goats as he was in the hearts of men.

What God wants—is *us*. But this requires that we willingly give ourselves to the Lord, holding nothing back. And so we offer the cup back to the Lord, saying, "Take this cup, take my life blood, take my heart and its desires, take my life."

Since this self-giving love is what we were created for, we will only find true joy when we give up ourselves in ways that will prove painful at the beginning but which will, in the end, produce the spiritual fruits of the life of Christ.

THE SACRIFICE OF THANKSGIVING

The cup we take is both the cup of suffering and the cup of blessing because it is the cup of Christ. As often as we eat the bread and drink the cup of the Eucharist, we proclaim Christ's death and resurrection. As often as we eat the bread of sorrow and drink the cup of woe, we partake of Christ.

But having received the cup of salvation, you must offer the sacrifice of praise and thanksgiving, for you must see God praised and thanked instead of yourself. But when you give yourself to God, you will discover that the fruit of self-sacrifice to the Lord is joy and love. Giving up ourselves to

Another, our greatest natural fear, turns out to be the road to human happiness and joy.

Knowing that in the taking of the cup we are also partaking of Christ, we give thanks. We do *not* give thanks for our suffering itself, which God abhors and has taken drastic measures to cure, but we *do* give thanks that Christ is in the cup of our suffering.

Having received the cup, and after God has begun his great transmutation of the suffering of our lives into the substance of his Son, we offer the cup back to God with thanks.

WE TAKE THE CUP AND OFFER IT TO THE FATHER

United to the redemptive life and ministry of Jesus Christ, the Christian who suffers is both priest and victim; both the one who sacrifices and the sacrifice which is offered; both the one who takes the cup and the one who offers it back to the Lord.

God's great plan of salvation, revealed through Saint Paul in his letter to the church in Ephesus, is revealed not only to us but *through* us: "Therefore be imitators of God as dear children. And walk in love, as Christ also has loved us and given Himself for us, an offering and a sacrifice to God for a sweet-smelling aroma" (Eph 5:1–2).

In suffering to redeem the world, we are imitators of God.

In emptying ourselves for the good of others, out of love, we are children of God.

In taking the cup which God offers and offering it back to him, we are imitators and children of God.

The Son of God came not to receive the sacrifices of men but to be the sacrifice for men. Baptized into Christ as members of his body, children of God, and inheritors of his kingdom, we, too, sacrifice ourselves for the life of the world. God has made himself the entire sacrificial and redemptive ministry necessary to save men: Jesus is at once the temple where God dwells with men, the Sacrifice for the sins of the world, and the Priest who offers that perfect sacrifice.

Christians enter into the divine liturgy, or offering, of which Christ is High Priest: "We have such a High Priest, who is seated at the right hand of the throne of the Majesty in the heavens, a Minister[29] of the sanctuary and of the true tabernacle which the Lord erected, and not man" (Heb 8:1–2).

29. Literally, "liturgist."

This is especially true in the liturgy of corporate worship, but the entire liturgy of life is offered up to God through Christ.

We must, therefore, with Jesus, offer ourselves to God as a living sacrifice. This means not merely bearing suffering stoically but actively offering it to God. It means giving ourselves to others in a sacrificial way that may cause us pain but which imitates God and proves us to be his loving sons and daughters renewed in his image.

Saint Paul says: "I have been crucified with Christ; it is no longer I who live, but Christ lives in me; and the life which I now live in the flesh I live by faith in the Son of God, who loved me and gave Himself for me" (Gal 2:20). This crucifying of self is an ongoing process: "For if you live according to the flesh you will die; but if by the Spirit you put to death the deeds of the body, you will live" (Rom 8:13).

This being crucified to Jesus is a painful process, just as Jesus's crucifixion was for him.

As priests who sacrifice themselves to God for his glory, out of love, we say: "This is my body. Take it and break it so that it can be reborn as Yours. Here is my life; it is being poured out into Your body, for Your glory. Distribute it to others so that they may have life through my life, which is now Your life. Take this cup, which is my life's blood, and make it Your life that I might truly live."

In this way, our sacrifice will be one with Christ's. It will also be one with all of the sacrifices of self that Christians have made for two thousand years and more. Then we will say, with Saint Paul and all the saints: "Yes, and if I am being poured out as a drink offering on the sacrifice and service of your faith, I am glad and rejoice with you all" (Phil 2:17).[30]

Willing to suffer with, through, for, and as Jesus Christ, we are able to join our sacrifice with his, becoming a partaker of the things of the altar. We partake of what Saint Paul teaches when he says:

> The cup of blessing which we bless, is it not the communion of the blood of Christ? The bread which we break, is it not the communion of the body of Christ? For we, though many, are one bread and one body; for we all partake of that one bread. Observe Israel after the flesh: Are not those who eat of the sacrifices partakers of the altar? (1 Cor 10:16–18)

---

30. See also 2 Timothy 4:16.

We say then with Christ in the Eucharist: "This is *my* body, this is *my* blood," because Christ is in us, and we are in him. But this is true only if I offer up my body and blood to him, for what he desires—is *me*!

When the bread is broken in the Eucharist, it is not only Christ's suffering and death that we remember but now our own, which is offered up with his. When the wine is poured in the cup we take, we partake of his blood, but we contribute our own which is now comingled with Christ's because we are his blood brothers and sisters and partakers of him.

In the Eucharist of the traditional *Book of Common Prayer*, we express this offering of ourselves to God through Christ in this way: "And here we offer and present unto thee, O Lord, our selves, our souls and bodies, to be a reasonable, holy, and living sacrifice unto thee."

Jesus continues to be the Temple, the High Priest, and the Sacrifice *through us*. Every time we suffer for Christ, we are applying his redemptive suffering on the cross, as well as his life, to a particular place and time, where he ministers through us!

And, therefore, we can accept what Saint Peter teaches us: "You also, as living stones, are being built up a spiritual house, a holy priesthood, to offer up spiritual sacrifices acceptable to God through Jesus Christ" (1 Pet 2:5).

With Christ, we take the cup of our life and offer it up to the Father as a living sacrifice.

> *O Lord and heavenly Father, we earnestly desire thy fatherly goodness, mercifully to accept this our sacrifice of praise and thanksgiving; most humbly beseeching thee to grant that, by the merits and death of thy Son Jesus Christ, and through faith in his blood, we, and all thy whole Church, may obtain remission of our sins, and all other benefits of his passion. And here we offer and present unto thee, O Lord, our selves, our souls and bodies, to be a reasonable, holy, and living sacrifice unto thee; humbly beseeching thee, that we may worthily receive the most precious Body and Blood of thy Son Jesus Christ, be filled with thy grace and heavenly benediction, and made one body with him, that he may dwell in us, and we in him. And although we are unworthy, through our manifold sins, to offer unto thee any sacrifice; yet we beseech thee to accept this our bounden duty and service; not weighing our merits, but pardoning our offences, through Jesus Christ our Lord; by whom, and with whom, in the unity of the Holy Ghost, all honour and glory be unto thee, O Father Almighty, world without end. Amen.* (Adapted from the Prayer of Oblation of the 1928 *Book of Common Prayer*)

CHAPTER 5

We Take the Cup and Find Christ in It

TAKE THIS CUP

When the Lord first offers us himself in suffering, saying, "take this cup," we find it too painful and unexpected, and we refuse. But out of love, the God who is supposedly not there shows up; the God who supposedly doesn't care is moved with compassion to deliver us from suffering; and the God who is supposedly too weak shows his strength and glory in becoming man and not only taking on all human suffering but also conquering all human enemies.

We rehearse, together, then, the gospel of suffering:

1. Far from being a sign of God's nonexistence, apathy, or impotence, human suffering is transformed by Christ's incarnation into a sign of God's presence, love, and power.

2. Because Christ has become man and suffered to redeem man, suffering is a primary means of participating in God's nature and being united to him.

3. As Christians partake of Christ and his suffering, their own suffering is transformed by God into glory and joy.

United to Jesus, who has taken the cup of suffering for us and transformed its evil into good, we find multiple reasons to rejoice in our suffering, in spite of its continuing evil and pain ("The Second Cup, Part III").

The Third Cup

This is the joy that God promises to us and on which we have meditated in this book. But where is the glory? The glory is in Christ, whose glory was first the cross, and then the resurrection and ascension. Our glory is Christ, but we are also his glory and his visible image in the world today. Truly partaking of Christ in his suffering and humiliation, we become partakers of his glory and exaltation, just as he has promised us.

Therefore, let us take the cup!

If God can transform water into wine, and himself into a man, then I'm certain he can transmute my suffering into glory and good (and me into his image).

Suffering becomes, for the Christian, a holy vocation, or calling. As Pope John Paul II has said:

> For it is above all a call. It is a vocation. Before all else he says: 'Follow me! Come! Take part through your suffering in this work of saving the world, a salvation achieved through my suffering! Through my cross.' Gradually, as the individual takes up his cross, spiritually uniting himself to the cross of Christ, the salvific meaning of suffering is revealed before him.[31]

I have to hold the cup, and *I* must lay hold of it. *I* must work out my salvation and take Christ and his cup with fear and trembling. *I* have to lift the cup in celebration and with cheers, giving thanks, not for my suffering but for how God has transformed it into a means of union with my Lord.

Together, *we* must drink the cup. Jesus is offering *us* a share in his kingdom, which is his life. Drinking together with Christ and his brothers and sisters is a sign of friendship, peace, and joy, while refusing to drink when offered the drink is to refuse intimacy with God himself.

We partake of a common cup, for there is one Christ of whom we have been made partakers. We drink it together, partaking of one another's suffering and joy; weeping with those who weep; and rejoicing with those who rejoice. Suffering with and for Jesus binds us together as blood brothers and sisters and a spiritual band of battle buddies.

The cup is Christ.

The cup is the cup of life and salvation that only comes through Christ's cross and our participation in it.

The cup of life, as we all know, contains an admixture of both humiliation and glory, of both sorrow and joy.

---

31. John Paul II, *Christian Meaning of Human Suffering*, 76.

But what we are left with in the end is this sweet taste: that what Satan and men mean for evil, God means for good.

What we get when we drink the cup of suffering with Jesus—*is Jesus!*

As the cup of self is emptied, God fills it with the Other, himself. It is a neverending cup, the miracle of the five thousand multiplied to the five thousandth power. This is the cup of suffering: we empty and deny ourselves, but only that God may completely fill us with himself. This self-emptying is painful, but it makes room for the joy, which is Christ and who is found in the cup he offers.

Sometimes we only see Jesus in the bottom of the cup, after we have partaken with faith.

"Take this cup," Jesus says, "the cup of suffering which I have transformed into the cup of salvation, the cup of my life and blood. I promise to be in the cup, offering you joy in my presence and glory in my kingdom."

Knowing that my suffering is itself still evil and nothing to be praised, I will, nevertheless, accept the suffering You have permitted me, as a means of grace and union with You.

Yes, Lord, I will take the cup, because You have asked me and because You have promised Yourself to me in it.

Taking the cup with Jesus, I discover what I could not know in any other way: that God has kept his promise to bring me glory and joy in Christ as I suffer with him.

For in suffering for Christ, I find union with God, the joy of all desiring.

> *Prayer: O Jesus, who, in Thy cruel Passion didst become the 'reproach of men and the Man of Sorrows,' I worship Thy divine Face. Once it shone with the beauty and sweetness of the Divinity; but now, for my sake, it is become as 'the face of a leper.' Yet, in that disfigured Countenance, I recognize Thy infinite love, and I am consumed with the desire of making Thee loved by all mankind. The tears that flowed so abundantly from Thy Eyes are to me as precious pearls that I delight to gather, that with their worth I may ransom the souls of poor sinners.*
>
> *O Jesus, whose Face is the sole beauty that ravishes my heart, I may not see here below the sweetness of Thy glance, nor feel the ineffable tenderness of Thy kiss, I bow to Thy Will—but I pray Thee to imprint in me Thy divine likeness, and I implore Thee so to inflame me with Thy love, that it may quickly consume me, and that I may soon reach the vision of Thy glorious Face in heaven. Amen.*
> (Therese of Lisieux)

APPENDIX

Joy and Glory in Other Passages

JOY IN SUFFERING IN THE BEATITUDES

The Beatitudes are a happy place to begin, for they proceed from the mouth of Jesus himself and are, in their very title, the Words of Blessing. The Beatitudes are God's word to us on how to be happy, that is, how to be joyful and blessed by God.

They are not what we expect.

At the center of the Beatitudes we find not self-esteem and earthly kingdoms, power, or glory: instead, we find suffering. Suffering, as we've defined it, is the lack of some good thing which we were created to enjoy. Listen again to the Words of Blessing: listen for the Gospel of Suffering.

> Blessed are the poor in spirit,
> For theirs is the kingdom of heaven.
> Blessed are those who mourn,
> For they shall be comforted.
> Blessed are the meek,
> For they shall inherit the earth.
> Blessed are those who hunger and thirst for righteousness,
> For they shall be filled.
> Blessed are the merciful,
> For they shall obtain mercy.
> Blessed are the pure in heart,

> For they shall see God.
> Blessed are the peacemakers,
> For they shall be called sons of God.
> Blessed are those who are persecuted for righteousness' sake,
> For theirs is the kingdom of heaven.
> Blessed are you when they revile and persecute you, and say all kinds of evil against you falsely for My sake. Rejoice and be exceedingly glad, for great *is* your reward in heaven, for so they persecuted the prophets who were before you. (Matt 5:3–12)

When Jesus stood on the mountain to give these words of life, he was also practicing to stand on the mount of Calvary. The Beatitudes are, as many have noticed, a new giving of the Law. But more than this, they are the self-giving of the Lawgiver himself. The Beatitudes are Christological in nature: they speak to us of Christ and life in him.

The crucifixion and the resurrection are, therefore, present together in the Beatitudes because the Beatitudes convey more than human words: they set before us the word of God himself. Jesus's words in the Beatitudes are not merely declaratory: they are also performative. He is not speaking abstract truths about the way to human happiness: he's offering participation in the very means to happiness. Jesus himself, and the word which proceeds from his mouth, is God's word to man: hear and accept him, and you will be blessed. As God the Father, on another mountain, the Mount of Transfiguration, says: "This is My beloved Son. Hear Him!" (Luke 9:35; Matt 17:5).

At the center of every one of these Words of Blessing is an oblation of self, a self-sacrifice which necessarily entails suffering of diverse kinds. The Gospel of Suffering is most pointed in verses 11 and 12: "Blessed are you when they revile and persecute you, and say all kinds of evil against you falsely for My sake. Rejoice and be exceedingly glad, for great is your reward in heaven, for so they persecuted the prophets who were before you."

When Christians think of suffering for Christ, they most naturally think of persecution. But, as we have said earlier, all Christian suffering matters, and not just persecution. Yet persecution is still the most salient form of Christian suffering and most clearly like the suffering of Christ. What does Jesus say about persecution from antichrists, knowing that he will experience the fullness of what he now offers his disciples?

He says, in essence, that of such are his kingdom. The person who is reviled and persecuted and to whom evil and suffering accrue *for Jesus's sake* is in a blessed state. This is plainly contrary to the surface level of our existence but just as plainly true in the spiritual level of existence on which

Jesus always speaks. While Jesus no doubt has other blessings in mind, the one he makes a point to mention is that such suffering for his sake should cause his disciples to rejoice and be exceedingly glad. It's not only that they *ought* to feel such joy: he commands that they have it, saying not "*Try* and rejoice" but "*Rejoice!*" and not "you *might be* exceedingly glad" but "*be* exceedingly glad." These are things he commands and not merely hypothetical responses.

This is similar language to the joy the Magi experienced on seeing the sign of Jesus Christ, when they "rejoiced with exceedingly great joy" (Matt 2:10). The sign which caused their rejoicing was the Star: *the sign which causes our rejoicing is the suffering we experience with and for Jesus.*

Jesus continues by saying that when we suffer for his sake, our reward in heaven is great. Heaven is the place where God dwells and the place of his blessing. It is not some far-off country in a galaxy far, far, away: heaven and earth meet in Jesus Christ, who has opened the kingdom of heaven to all believers. This joy, therefore, although it is eschatological in its fullness, is a joy of which Christians partake in this life. This must be so, for we partake of Jesus in this life through suffering, and where Jesus is, we shall always find men rejoicing with exceedingly great joy.

What is this reward? It is all that God has ever promised to his children, but most especially our reward is this: God himself.

The Beatitudes apply first and foremost to Jesus himself. *He* is the Reviled and Persecuted Man; he is the one against whom false things were said and done. He is not only the prophets or messengers but also the Son of the Vinedresser. The Beatitudes apply to every Christian man because they were first lived out by the Man, Jesus Christ.

JOY IN SUFFERING IN THE JAMES 1:2-4

Saint James begins his letter not with a whimper but a bang: "My brethren, count it all joy when you fall into various trials, knowing that the testing of your faith produces patience. But let patience have *its* perfect work, that you may be perfect and complete, lacking nothing" (Jas 1:2-4).

Not designed, perhaps, to win friends and influence people, James's introduction to his letter is, nevertheless, the Gospel of Suffering, which he must have learned from his brother and Lord. In James, we discover another mention of the trials of life we will face and another commandment to rejoice in these trials.

Appendix

James provides us with a Christian moral theology in these verses. The reason James gives why we should count our trials joy is because trials test our faith. This testing of faith has at least two related meanings. On the one hand, trials test our faith to see if it is genuine. If our faith melts away, and we retreat from God when we suffer, then our faith is weak or not genuine. If, however, we discover that we love God even when he allows good things to be taken from us, then our faith is discovered to be genuine and strong.

Suffering, or trials, also test faith in that they refine and purify it. The act of suffering has the potential to produce holiness, a holiness that comes from the fire which is God's Holy Spirit. Even the Son himself was purified by what he suffered, for the writer of the book of Hebrews writes: "though He was a Son, *yet* He learned obedience by the things which He suffered" (Heb 5:8). For when we pass through the fire of suffering, that which is impure is burned up, while that which is holy and given to God remains.

God is a living, refining fire (Mal 2:2–3) and a consuming fire (Deut 4:34; Heb 12:29). What makes us so certain that coming into the presence of this God is always a pleasant thing? It certainly won't be pleasant for those on the wrong side of the Great Assize. And even holy Isaiah had his lips burned with a living coal when he entered into the presence of God.

Saint Peter, as well, speaks of the testing of our faith by trials and the joy that comes from discovering that our faith is genuine. He says: "In this you greatly rejoice, though now for a little while, if need be, you have been grieved by various trials, that the genuineness of your faith, *being* much more precious than gold that perishes, though it is tested by fire, may be found to praise, honor, and glory at the revelation of Jesus Christ" (1 Pet 1:6–7).

The writer of the hymn "How Firm a Foundation" understood these things as well and put them in a memorable form for us:

> When through the deep waters I call thee to go,
> The rivers of sorrow shall not overflow;
> For I will be with thee thy troubles to bless
> And sanctify to thee thy deepest distress.
>
> When through fiery trials thy pathway shall lie,
> My grace, all-sufficient, shall be thy supply.
> The flames shall not hurt thee; I only design
> Thy dross to consume and thy gold to refine.

James continues his catechesis on Christian perfection. One of the blessings of trials, in which we rejoice, is that the testing of our faith by trials produces in us "patience" or "endurance." This endurance is essential because it is related to our abiding in Christ. If our response to the trials God permits in our lives is to back away from God or to doubt him, then we lack the ability to endure suffering for the Jesus who endured suffering for us. To the degree that Christ is in us and loved by us, we will endure our sufferings precisely because we recognize our Lord in them. Recognizing Jesus in our suffering, we see in our afflictions His scarred hands and wounded side and cry with Thomas: "My Lord and my God!"

To lack endurance is to be willing to see God when things are good (defined as "going according to my will and plan") but not when things are "bad." The ironic thing is that such people rarely see God in good things either since they assume things are going well because *their* will and plans have obtained their blessing.

To be patient and enduring is to entrust yourself to God and his plan for blessing you and to not trust too much in yourself. To be patient is to recognize your dependence on God for every blessing. These are the very things God desires for us and which constitute our blessing: that we trust God and his will in our lives.

This endurance is all-important to our life in Christ. Our growth as Christians is a slow growth, like the biological growth of a human, which takes eighteen years or more to come to perfection. A constant life of abiding patiently in Christ will lead to Christlike growth, maturity, and perfection. But think of what happens when the process of growth is constantly interrupted: life withers or at best remains immature in substance, even when mature in years

When we endure the trials in our lives as what they truly are—partaking of the sufferings of Christ and thereby attaining union with him—then they become occasions of the blessing which comes from being in the presence of God. Being found in the presence of God and receiving his bountiful blessing of himself, we rejoice!

James continues his teaching on trials and blessing in verse 12, when he says: "Blessed *is* the man who endures temptation; for when he has been approved, he will receive the crown of life which the Lord has promised to those who love Him."

We usually imagine this crown of life to be entirely future. While undoubtedly we will receive the fullness of this crown of life only in the life to come, the thrust of James's very practical letter seems to be on how to live a godly and wise life *in this world*.

Any time we come across a phrase such as "the crown of life," we are likely to imagine some particular kind of reward God has in mind for us. This may remain vague or may be imagined as long life, health, lack of sorrow, rest from our labors, peace, etc. How much more profitable (and probably more accurate) it is to imagine the promised crown of life to be Jesus himself! What reward could possibly be greater? What reward is more fitting for those who, like Christ and with Christ, endure the trials for the glory of the Lord set before them!

GLORY IN SUFFERING IN PHILIPPIANS 3:10-11

When we come to the third chapter of Saint Paul's letter to the church at Philippi, we must come remembering Paul's great hymn to Christ, which we find in his second chapter.

> Let this mind be in you which was also in Christ Jesus, who, being in the form of God, did not consider it robbery to be equal with God, but made Himself of no reputation, taking the form of a bondservant, and coming in the likeness of men. And being found in appearance as a man, He humbled Himself and became obedient to the point of death, even the death of the cross. Therefore God also has highly exalted Him and given Him the name which is above every name, that at the name of Jesus every knee should bow, of those in heaven, and of those on earth, and of those under the earth, and that every tongue should confess that Jesus Christ is Lord, to the glory of God the Father. (Phil 2:5-11)

This mind is the mind of humility that characterized everything Jesus did. From our earlier discussion of Christ's entire life of suffering, we should quickly recognize that this humility of Christ in giving up himself as a sacrifice for our good is inseparable from his suffering. Depriving himself for our sake of every good to which he had a right, Jesus suffered for us.

Paul summarizes the humiliation of Christ in terms of his incarnation, his life of service and obedience, and his death on the cross for us. The starting point for following Christ in his life is his humiliation and suffering. Having been baptized into Christ, including not only his resurrection and life but also his suffering and death, we live out the life of Christ in us. Following Christ in all things, and being in Christ and having him be in us, we must humble ourselves and suffer: we must humble ourselves to the point of death and the giving up of all things.

But since the suffering of Christ and Christians is never mere suffering, Paul explains the teleology of Christian suffering: glory. Paul begins verse 9 with one of his characteristic "therefores." "Therefore"—*as a result*—of Christ's humiliation and suffering, God has highly exalted him. Paul doesn't bother to explain how or why this is but merely asserts this most fundamental of Christian beliefs and creeds: that as a result of Jesus's humbling himself in his incarnation, life, and death, the Father has exalted him. Once again, we discover that Jesus's suffering and crucifixion are inseparable from his resurrection.

Jesus is exalted so that his Name is above every other name, and he is acknowledged by all to be Lord. By this, the Father is also glorified, just as Jesus was glorified by his being lifted up not only from the tomb but also on the cross.

With Philippians 2 as our context, let us now read Philippians 3:8–11.

> Indeed, I count everything as loss because of the surpassing worth of knowing Christ Jesus my Lord. For his sake I have suffered the loss of all things and count them as rubbish, in order that I may gain Christ and be found in him, not having a righteousness of my own that comes from the law, but that which comes through faith in Christ, the righteousness from God that depends on faith— that I may know him and the power of his resurrection, and may share his sufferings, becoming like him in his death, that by any means possible I may attain the resurrection from the dead.

Paul begins this passage by affirming his union with and participation in Christ. The goal, for Paul, is knowledge of Christ, gaining Christ, and being found in Christ. These are all ways of saying "union with Christ" or "partaking of Christ." Notice, especially, the implied means by which Paul will so gain Christ and be one with him: suffering.

This implied suffering is expressed in verse 8 in two different phrases. First, Paul says that he counts everything as loss because of the surpassing worth of knowing Christ. Paul perpetually declares and acts upon his intention to give up all things for the sake of Christ. This giving up of all things is in imitation of and in union with the Christ of Philippians 2, who made himself of no reputation and humbled himself in every imaginable way. Paul also proclaims that he has suffered the loss of all things in order to gain Christ.

APPENDIX

Here is the Christlike pattern again: suffer (give up all things) and receive the glory of the Lord (Christ himself). What is this loss of all things of which Paul speaks, but suffering? And what does it gain but glory, the glory which is Christ himself?

In verses 10–11, Paul further reinforces this basic pattern of coming to Christ through suffering that we might partake of his glory. The goal of Paul's life in these verses closely mimics the life of Christ in Philippians 2.

Paul's desire that he may "share his sufferings" (verse 10) is the partaking of Christ's self-emptying of Philippians 2.

Paul's "becoming like him in his death" (verse 10) is the partaking of Christ's death in Philippians 2, "He humbled himself and became obedient to the point of death, even the death of the cross."

Paul's "that by any means possible I may attain the resurrection from the dead" (verse 11) is the partaking of Christ's exaltation in Philippians 2: "Therefore God also has highly exalted Him and given Him the name which is above every name."

Paul's path to glory is Christ's path to glory, done in union with Christ: first, the suffering of humbling self and giving up all things in life, then the ultimate self-emptying and suffering of death, and finally, the resultant glory of the resurrected life of Jesus Christ.

This same lesson is even written in our bodies, according to Saint Paul. For in verse 21, he professes that Jesus: "will transform our lowly body that it may be conformed to His glorious body." Lowliness to glory: that is the Gospel of Suffering that we live out in Christ as members of his Body.

GLORY IN SUFFERING IN HEBREWS 2:8–11

> For in that He put all in subjection under him, He left nothing that is not put under him. But now we do not yet see all things put under him. But we see Jesus, who was made a little lower than the angels, for the suffering of death crowned with glory and honor, that He, by the grace of God, might taste death for everyone. For it was fitting for Him, for whom are all things and by whom are all things, in bringing many sons to glory, to make the captain of their salvation perfect through sufferings. For both He who sanctifies and those who are being sanctified are all of one, for which reason He is not ashamed to call them brethren (Heb 2:8–11).

All of Hebrews 2 speaks of Christ's humiliation and suffering, which is, at the same time, an expression of the glory of his divine nature, the means to the glorification of his human nature, and the means to our glorification in him.

In speaking of the Son's glory, which surpasses that of angels (Heb 1), the writer of Hebrews proclaims how it is precisely in the Son's suffering, in the form of taking on human nature, that his glory is manifested to the creation. When the writer of the book of Hebrews quotes David from Psalm 8—"You have made him a little lower than the angels; You have crowned him with glory and honor"—are not both David and the writer of Hebrews expressing the Gospel of Suffering? An intrinsic relationship exists between humiliation and condescension, which are forms of suffering, and the glory that is given to Christ in his human nature.

The tension inherent in the Gospel of Suffering is expressed in verse 8 of Hebrews 2: "But now we do not yet see all things put under him." Because of Jesus's coming as the Suffering Servant, he is exalted as the King of Glory. And yet, although in one sense Jesus is already reigning, we do not yet see all things put under him. The list of things not yet completely under the reign of Christ should include our human suffering. Although God incarnates himself in our human suffering and is even now transforming it into glory, we do not yet see suffering completely put under Christ's feet, any more than we completely see sin, death, and the devil completely subdued.

One of the clearest expressions of the Gospel of Suffering, in addition to 2 Corinthians 4:17, is Hebrew 2:9: "But we see Jesus, who was made a little lower than the angels, for the suffering of death crowned with glory and honor, that He, by the grace of God, might taste death for everyone."

The writer of Hebrews interprets the "man" who is made lower than the angels to be Jesus Christ, and not human nature in general. Of course, the two are ultimately one, because Jesus is the Second Adam or Second "Man," in which the new humanity in Christ subsists. This profound act of humility and humiliation, this voluntarily giving up of some good to which he had a right, is the beginning of the suffering of Christ. The Jesus of Hebrews 2 who makes himself a little lower than the angels is the Jesus of Philippians 2 who "made Himself of no reputation, taking the form of a bondservant, and coming in the likeness of men."

It was precisely because of this emptying of self, the writer of Hebrews asserts, that Jesus was crowned with glory and honor. The making himself lower than the angels and taking on human nature is the same kind of self-giving suffering and sacrifice as that of the suffering of death which Jesus experienced. The end of this suffering is glory and honor.

Jesus humbled himself and suffered so that his human nature might be glorified. But this glory he receives as a consequence of his suffering is not only for himself: he took on human nature, and suffered and died in it, that he might glorify those who are in him as members of his Body and partakers of the New Man.

In verse 10, we read that "in bringing many sons to glory," the Father made Jesus "perfect through suffering." This verse can't mean that through suffering Jesus arrived at some moral perfection which he did not have before, for he was already perfect in this sense. And yet if Jesus came to take on himself the afflictions of mankind, over the course of time he, in his time-bound human nature, had to actually experience the sufferings of mankind.

Jesus is the perfect man, not only in terms of his innate moral perfection but also in his perfectly obeying the will of the Father and in his perfectly suffering. Jesus "perfectly" suffered, both in the sense that he took upon himself all human suffering and also in the sense that he suffered perfectly—by not blaming the Father and by not complaining, but by offering his suffering up to the Father as a perfect sacrifice of self.

Jesus, in his human nature, has experienced all human experience perfectly, including both suffering and death. Perfectly experiencing the evil of human deprivation, he turned it into the supreme Good. Perfectly suffering the griefs and pains of human affliction, he was joyful. Perfectly experiencing human death, he triumphed over it. Once again, we see this summary of the Gospel of Suffering: that what wicked creatures mean for evil, God means for good. God transforms evil, or suffering, into good, the good which God calls glory and joy.

BIBLIOGRAPHY

Coffman, Elesha. "Beyond Pearl Harbor: How God Caught Up with the Man Who Led Japan's Surprise Attack." *Christianity Today*, August 8, 2008. http://www.christianitytoday.com/history/2008/august/beyond-pearl-harbor.html.

John Paul II, Pope. *On the Christian Meaning of Human Suffering*. Anniversary ed. Boston: Pauline, 2014.

Keller, Timothy. *The Reason for God: Belief in an Age of Skepticism*. Reprint, New York: Penguin, 2009.

Lewis, C. S. *Mere Christianity*. New York: HarperCollins, 2001.

———. *The Problem of Pain*. New York: Harper, 2001.

Lubac, Henri de. *History and Spirit: The Understanding of Scripture According to Origen*. San Francisco: Ignatius, 2007.

Mascall, E. L. *Christ, the Christian, and the Church: A Study of the Incarnation and Its Consequences*. London: Longmans, 1946.

"Mistuo Fuchida." https://en.wikipedia.org/wiki/Mitsuo_Fuchida.

Sheen, Fulton. *Life of Christ*. New York: Image, 1977.

———. *The Mystical Body of Christ: A Timeless Portrait of the Church from a Beloved Catholic Evangelist*. Notre Dame: Christian Classics, 2015.

Stevenson, James. *A New Eusebius: Documents Illustrating the History of the Church to AD 337*. Revised by W. H. C. Frend. London: SPCK, 1987.

West, Christopher. *Theology of the Body Explained: A Commentary on John Paul II's "Gospel of the Body."* Boston: Pauline, 2003.

Wright, N. T. *Surprised by Hope: Rethinking Heaven, the Resurrection, and the Mission of the Church*. New York: Harper, 2008.

SUBJECT INDEX

1984, 65

Adam and Eve, 27, 65, 77, 168
"Ah, Holy Jesus," 27–28
altar, 67, 147, 177
anamnesis, 141
angel, suffering as, 139–140
angels, 32, 101, 116, 131, 138
Angelus, 17
apostles, 47, 105
Aslan, 39
Athanasius, Saint, 49

baptism, 51, 53–56, 58, 61, 63, 69, 120–121, 127, 173–174, 176
Beatific Vision, 37, 72
Beatitudes, 182–185
Bible, 46–47, 87–88, 140
blood, 4, 13–14, 70, 119, 161–162, 175, 177–178, 180–181
body, 16, 32, 37, 47, 54, 59, 78, 80, 93, 122, 128, 138, 190
Body of Christ, 46–51, 54, 59, 61–64, 68–69, 74–75, 77–78, 80, 92, 102, 106, 122, 134, 138, 170
Book of Common Prayer, 36, 54, 57, 73, 138, 141–142, 174, 178
bread, 64–72, 141–142, 167, 177–178
Buddha, 1

Chalcedon, Council of, 15
chiaroscuro, 151
children, 102, 109–110, 114, 130–131, 140

children of God, 61–69-70, 75, 109–111, 114–116, 134, 167, 176
Christus Victor, 99
Chrysostom, Saint, 100
church, 46–52, 55, 59, 61, 63–65, 74–82, 92–93, 105–107, 120–122, 133–135, 138, 157, 169–170
"Circumcision of Christ, The" (poem), 20
coinherence, 126
Collect for Easter Even, 36
communion of saints, 120–121
community, 77–78, 123
compassion, 127–129, 131, 179
consolation, 126, 131–133, 138
Corinthian church, 122, 132
Creed, 120
cross of Christ—see Jesus Christ, Crucifixion
crosses, 2–3, 32–33, 39, 74–75, 80, 123, 129, 145, 146, 166, 168, 173
crown, 35, 126, 187–188
crucifix, 145, 165
crucifying self, 77, 169, 177

David, 110
DeShazer, Jacob, 137
Didache, 65
dissatisfaction, 149–150
Donne, John, 103, 123–124
Doolittle's Raiders, 137

earthen vessels, 75, 92–93
ecclesiology, 48
endurance, 105, 187

Subject Index

Erlandson, Charles, 62, 75, 112
Eucharist, 20, 36, 49, 55–56, 63–68,
    71–73, 121, 137–138, 141–142,
    147, 175, 178
evil, x, xi, 11–13, 16, 18, 24–25, 29–31,
    59–61, 69, 76, 101, 107, 114,
    121, 147, 150, 162, 168, 172,
    179, 181, 184, 192
evil into good, xi, 11–13, 16, 17, 29–30,
    58–60, 64, 73, 76, 96, 114, 172,
    179, 181, 192
exaltation, 90n, 135, 144, 180

faith, 13, 40–41, 88, 107, 146, 157, 170,
    177, 181, 186–187
food, 27, 65–66, 68, 70
forgetting, 140
forgiveness, 168
Francis, S. Trevor, 152
Fuchida, Mitsuo, 137

garden, 4, 26–27, 32, 71, 101, 102, 145,
    168, 173
Garden of Eden, 7
Garden of Gethsemane, 5, 26, 27, 66, 99,
    144, 164–167
Galilee, 21
giving of self, 3, 13, 19, 22, 67, 70–71,
    77, 93, 115, 117, 119–122, 125–
    126, 128, 130, 132, 135, 138,
    161, 164, 175, 177, 189
Gloria, The, 158
glory, xi, 1, 8, 11, 30–39, 56, 81, 87–96,
    88n, 92n, 97, 98, 101–103, 105,
    111, 114–117, 119, 126, 135,
    146–148, 151, 154–155, 157,
    161, 168, 171–173, 180–181,
    190–191
"Glory be to Jesus," 13–14
Good Friday, 18

Check the form on God and subentries
God:
    blessings of, 3, 72, 130, 133, 135, 183
    calling, 170
    commandment, 87–89, 96

compassion, 131–132, 179
condemnation, 170
consuming fire, 186
deliverance, 23
discipline, 69, 109–111, 113
face of, 38
fire, 186
forgiveness, 167–168
glory of, 36–38, 73, 90, 92–93, 101,
    111, 114–116, 147, 153–1578
goodness, x, 11, 13, 16, 94, 149–151,
    162, 172, 192
grace, 116, 130, 190–191
holiness, 111
judgment, 26, 29, 70, 140
kingdom, 34, 38, 129, 166–168, 184
love, 11–12, 15–16, 30, 37, 67, 74,
    94, 118–119, 138, 165, 170
mercy, 127, 132, 139
mountain, 39
mysteries, 61, 130, 156
nature, 65
nature, partaking of, 8, 39, 45, 53
plan of salvation, 116
power, 1–2
presence, 8, 32, 65, 69, 140, 166, 186
promises, 14, 91, 146–147, 173, 180
punishment, 31, 69,
righteousness, 111
self-revelation, 36, 37, 144, 155
simplicity, 11

gospel of suffering, xi, 3, 8, 33, 65,
    87–89, 91, 94–96, 110, 132, 136,
    139, 153, 179, 183–185, 190–192
grace, see God, grace
Gregory of Nazianzus, 15, 2

hauntedness of man, 149–150
heaven, 48, 72, 97, 100–101, 127, 138,
    140, 144, 146–147, 151, 164–
    167, 185
Herbert, George, 164
Herod, 34, 99
Holy Communion, see Eucharist
"How Firm a Foundation," 186

Subject Index

humbling self, 40, 93–94, 129, 135, 188–190
humiliation, 31, 33–34, 90n, 97, 121, 123, 135, 144, 180, 188
"Humbly I Adore Thee" (Thomas Aquinas), 40–41

i am the moon, but YOU ARE the Sun, 155
image of God, 30, 92n, 114, 119, 155,
incarnation, see Jesus Christ, incarnation
Institutes of Christian Religion (Calvin), 61
Isaac, 38, 67, 175

Jesus Christ
    ascension, 47, 58, 72, 92, 142, 180
    baptism, 38, 51, 53–56, 58, 61, 63, 69, 74, 120–121, 127, 153, 173–174
    birth, 19, 32, 72
    body and blood, 64–65, 68, 73, 77, 163, 178
    Bread of Life, 19, 63, 69, 70–72, 143, 165
    circumcision, 20
    cross, 2–6, 16–21, 23–25, 30, 32–37, 39–40, 49, 55, 59, 61, 63–64, 67, 72–76, 79–80, 82–83, 92, 95, 100–102, 114, 127, 129, 139, 144–146, 148, 150, 165–168, 173, 180, 188, 189,
    crucifixion, 15, 18, 22, 24, 30, 33–36, 39–40, 55, 58, 64, 72, 95, 101–102, 129, 144–148, 156, 165–167, 173, 177, 184, 189
    Daily Bread, 71, 142, 167, 173
    eucharistic body, 49, 63–64
    exaltation, 189–190
    feeding of the five thousand, 83, 92, 128, 138, 181
    firstborn, 116
    glorification, 33, 35, 153, 156–157, 189–191
    glory, 61, 65, 75, 79, 94–95
    Good Shepherd, 27, 38, 83, 109, 111
    high priestly prayer, 155
    holiness, 69, 101, 109, 186
    human nature, 31, 33, 45–51, 54–55, 58, 63, 115–116, 144, 169, 191–192
    humiliation, 19, 23–24, 33–35, 39, 81, 92, 97, 105, 135, 145, 180, 188–189, 191
    humility, 19, 21, 34, 188, 191–192
    image of Christ, 113–117
    incarnation, 15–18, 32, 39, 45–47, 55, 61, 71–72, 94, 96, 104, 120, 170, 179, 188–189
    king, 34, 139, 144, 165–166
    Messiah, 3, 34
    mystical body, 46–52, 59, 63, 73, 76, 81, 93, 102, 105, 134, 138, 145, 153
    New Man, 55–56, 76, 101, 114, 118, 146
    obedience, 16, 21–22, 26, 30, 71, 100, 108, 110, 112, 165–167, 169, 186, 188, 192
    perfection, 16, 21–23, 33, 72, 77, 117, 169, 190, 192
    reign, 51, 100, 191
    resurrection, 10, 15–16, 36, 38, 40, 48, 55, 60–66, 72, 82, 88n, 92, 100–102, 107, 138, 142, 144–148, 156, 166, 173, 175, 190
    Second Adam, 16, 26, 32, 58–59, 77, 102, 168, 169
    Suffering Servant, 3, 19, 30, 33–34, 38, 70, 125, 136, 142, 146, 165, 191
    Theologian's Stone, 30
    trial, 23, 34, 102
    True Alchemist, 30
    weeps, 127–128
John, Saint, 136, 170
John Paul II, 108, 170, 180
Joseph (patriarch), 13, 30, 107
joy (rejoice), 8, 15, 31, 33–34, 36, 60, 69, 87–90, 94–158, 172–176, 179–181, 183, 185–186, 192
joy and glory in suffering passages, 90n
judgment, 25, 29, 55, 69, 102

Subject Index

justification, 36, 101–102, 146

Keble, John, 20, 47
Keller, Tim, 126–127
a Kempis, Thomas, 98
Kingdom of God, see God, kingdom

Last Supper, 26–27, 156
Lewis, C.S., 141, 146–147
liturgy, 71, 176–177
Lord's Prayer, 71, 153, 162–168
Lord's Supper, see Eucharist
love, 13, 54, 70, 77–78, 82–83, 117, 119, 122, 125–127, 129, 161–162, 166, 175–176, 186
    "Love Divine, All Loves Excelling," 118
Love Me, Love My Wife, 134n
Loyal Temperance Union, 73
de Lubac, Henri, 82
Luther, Martin, 3

Magi, 154, 185
Marriage Feast of the Lamb, 46, 49, 72
Martha, 147
Mascall, E.L., 51
memorial, 141–142
miracles, 16, 29, 65
mnemonic device, 140–141
moral theology, 186
Muirhead, Lionel, 52

Nathanael, 20
nature, 66
Nazareth, 20–21,
new birth, 59–60
New Creation, 20, 32, 55, 59
New Heavens and New Earth, 57, 147
New Man, 47, 55–56, 59, 114

Oblation, Prayer of, 178
offering, 67, 83, 133, 163–165, 174–178
O'Connor, Flannery, 146
"O Sacred Head, Sore Wounded," 6
"O the Deep, Deep Love of Jesus," 151–152

Palm Sunday, 34
pain, xi, 1, 23–24, 59–61, 69, 75, 78, 81, 83, 90, 104–105, 109–111, 113–114, 117, 121–123, 131n, 139, 141, 145–146, 149–151, 157, 161, 163, 167, 175, 117, 179, 181, 192
Paul, Saint, 47, 60, 77–78, 94, 105–107, 122, 125–126, 132, 134–136, 145, 156–157, 189–190
Peter, 2–3, 21, 23, 39, 133, 144–145, 172
perichoresis, 126
persecution, 184
Philippian church, 126
    Polycarp, 136–137
poor, 128
postmodernism, 22
prayer, 5, 71, 110, 132–134, 164–168
Prayer (I), (George Herbert), 164
prosperity gospel, 3,

recapitulation, 16, 19, 26, 47n, 58, 77, 105, 114
reconciliation, 121–123
redemption, 2, 8, 12–13, 15–19, 24, 26–27, 31, 45–46, 51, 53, 56–57, 59, 72–73, 75, 77, 79, 81–83, 96, 104–108, 154, 169–171, 174, 176, 179
resurrection, 36, 55, 60, 66, 80, 114, 139, 146
Rembrandt, 151
reward, 184–185, 188

sacrament, 31–32, 37, 40, 59, 65–66, 70, 74, 123, 138, 147, 155
sacrifice, 3–4, 26, 66–68, 70–71, 77, 117, 128 133, 142, 164, 168–169, 174–178, 184
salvation, plan of, 88n, 116, 176
sanctification, 51, 114
Satan, 2, 4–5, 30–31, 35, 55, 69, 99–101, 168
scientism, 65
serving others, 130–131, 133, 170
Sheen, Fulton, 50–51, 66–67, 144
Simon of Cyrene, v, 80, 129

Subject Index

sin, 2, 7, 150–151
smartphone, 140
Smytton, George Hunt, 171
spirituality, 47
Star Trek, 65
Stephen, Saint, 47, 136
"Strife is O'er, The," 148
suffering for others, 94, 107–108, 112, 117, 125–138, 176–177
suffering of others, 79–80, 123, 169
sun, 65, 115, 155
sympathy, 127–129

theodicy, x-xi
theology of glory, 3
Therese of Lisieux, 181
Time Bandits, 24
Tree of Life, 24, 32–33, 35, 102, 173
trials, 58, 78, 89, 154, 157, 185–186

Trinity, 11, 16, 29, 39–40, 55, 78, 119–122, 126

union with God (Christ), 13, 15–16, 24, 31, 33, 36, 39, 45–47, 53–56, 61, 69, 91n, 97–99, 104, 118, 120–121, 132, 136, 140, 162–164, 169, 180–181, 187, 189–190
unity, 80, 119–122
Upper Room, 38

vocation, suffering as, 180

war, 119
Williams, Charles, 126
wine, 16, 20, 25–27, 64–73, 141–142, 167, 174, 178
word of God, 184
Wright, N.T., 82

SCRIPTURE INDEX

Genesis
3	120
22:7	175
50:20	13, 30

Deuteronomy
4:34	186
7:22	114
21:23	24

Leviticus
19:11	70

1 Kings
1:6	110

Psalms
8	191
22	34
75:8	24

Proverbs
25:2	97

Isaiah
51:17	25
53	34
53:5	59

Jeremiah
25:15–28	25

Zechariah
9:9	34

Malachi
2:2–3	186

Matthew
2:2	34
2:10	154, 185
2:23	21
5:3–12	182–183
5:3	35
5:10	35
5:16	153
9:36	128
14:14	128
15:32	128
16:21	144
17:5	184
18:21–35	129
18:27	128
19:17	11
20	64
20:34	128
21:5	34
21:9	34
25:34–40	133–134
26	64, 134
26:26	71
27:11	34
27:29	34
27:39–40	5
27:42	5, 34

Scripture Index

Mark

1:41	128
8:31–33	2
8:34–35	3
9	56
10	55
10:38–39	56

Luke

1:46–55	95
2:12	20
2:51	21
4:29	21
9:35	184
12:40	55
19:41	127
22:17–18	26
22:19	141
22:42	5, 21, 26
22:44	5, 24
24:26	33

John

2:22	147
3:16	12
4:34	21, 71
6:12	83
6:38	21
8:28	35, 38
11:40	147
12:16	147
12:23	35
12:24–25	66–67
12:27–28	35, 156N
13:17	27
13:31–32	156N
14:9	38, 165
16:20–21	59
17:1–5	156
19:28–29	26–27
19:41	32, 145
20:15	32
21:17–19	156N

Acts

1–2	46–47
1:1	47
5:41	105
7:55–60	136
7:60	47
9:4	47
9:15–16	105–106
9:16	60
12:5	133
14:19–20	60
14:22	61
16:25	136
20:35	129

Romans

5:2	117
5:3–5	117–118
6:3–5	53–54
6:23	151
8:13–17	115
8:13	177
8:18	151
8:22–23	59
8:22	149
8:28–30	116
8:29	61, 116
8:37	97
12	54
12:15	78

1 Corinthians

2:16	117
4:1	130
6	54
6:19–20	59, 153
9:13	67
10:16–18	177
10:31	153
11:7	115
11:23–26	174
11:26	67
12	54, 121–122
12:26	122
15:21	16

2 Corinthians

1:3–11	131–132
2:5	122
3	91–92
3:18	117
4:3–4	91n
4:6	92N
4:7–11	91
4:7	93
4:10–11	106
4:10	93, 138
4:11–15	127
4:11–12	125
4:15	125
4:17	94, 191
4:18	94
6:4–10	106
7:8–11	122
11:1	133
11:7	135
11:23–29	60, 107
11:29	77
12:15	125

Galatians

2:20	177
3:13	24
4:4–5	16
6:9–10	130

Ephesians

1:6, 12, 14	153
2:6	97
3:10–13	156
3:21	157
4:4–6	121
4:12	134
5	54
5:1–2	176

Philippian

1:21–26	126
1:29	77
2	134–135, 189–190
2:5–11	188
2:5–10	117
2:6–9	19
2:8–10	30, 33
2:17	126, 177
3:7–11	107
3:8–11	189
3:10–11	60–61, 188–190
3:10	74–75, 138
4:14	122

Colossians

1:5	38
1:15	115, 116
1:20	173
1:24	80–82
1:27	117

Hebrews

1	191
1:3	115, 116
1:5–6	116
2:8–11	190–192
2:9	33, 116
2:10	117, 173
2:17	16
4:15	127
5:8	21, 186
8:1–2	176
9	70
12:5–11	109–111
12:7–11	69
12:29	186

James

1:2–4	185–188
1:9	135

1 Peter

1:6–9	157
2:5	178
2:24	59
3:18	23
4:12–19	89–90
4:12–14	154
4:13	173

Scripture Index

1 Peter (*continued*)

4:16	154
5:9–11	79

2 Peter

2:14	46

Revelation

1:13–15	155
19:6	46
21:2–3	46

www.ingramcontent.com/pod-product-compliance
Lightning Source LLC
Chambersburg PA
CBHW060606230426
43670CB00011B/1999